CHUCK JAFFE'S
LIFETIME GUIDE
TO MUTUAL FUNDS

T0346276

OTHER BOOKS BY CHARLES A. JAFFE

The Right Way to Hire Financial Help

CHUCK JAFFE'S
LIFETIME GUIDE TO MUTUAL FUNDS

AN OWNER'S MANUAL

CHARLES A. JAFFE

BASIC
BOOKS

A Member of the Perseus Books Group
New York

Many of the designations used by manufacturers and sellers to distinguish their products are claimed as trademarks. Where those designations appear in this book and Basic Books was aware of a trademark claim, the designations have been printed in initial capital letters.

Copyright 2000 by Charles A. Jaffe
Previously published by Perseus Publishing
Published by Basic Books, A Member of the Perseus Books Group

All rights reserved. No part of this publication may be reproduced, stored in a retrieval system, or transmitted, in any form or by any means, electronic, mechanical, photocopying, recording, or otherwise, without the prior written permission of the publisher. Printed in the United States of America.

Cataloging-in-Publication Data is available from the Library of Congress.
ISBN 0–7382-0273-8

Find us on the World Wide Web at http://www.basicbooks.com

Books published by Basic Books are available at special discounts for bulk purchases in the U.S. by corporations, institutions, and other organizations. For more information, please contact the Special Markets Department at The Perseus Books Group, 11 Cambridge Center, Cambridge, MA 02141, or call 617/252-5298 or 800/255-1514, or e-mail special.markets@perseusbooks.com

Text design by Jeff Williams
Set in 11-point Palatino by Perseus Publishing Services
First printing, October 2000

For Susan (who is my *lifetime guide),*
Thomson and Whitney, and my parents

CONTENTS

Part 2: When You Own

Part 3: When You Sell

ACKNOWLEDGMENTS

That's my name and face on the cover of this book, but it didn't get there without a lot of help.

For starters, there is Karl Weber, my agent, who took a raw project proposal that wasn't particularly good and helped turn it into the framework for what I believe is an outstanding book.

Jacqueline Murphy, my editor at Perseus Books, always gave me the feeling that she was more excited about this project than I was. Real or imagined—and I was pretty darned happy when this book was near completion—her energy for the book was a real motivator. The best moment of the whole writing process may have been when I learned that she actually liked what I had turned in.

Then there is the home team: My father, brother, and father-in-law all slogged through a big partial draft of the book and confirmed for me that the concept worked. What's more, their suggestions improved the finished product. My wife, Susan, got the one job in this project that I really did not want to do myself, namely calling all of the toll-free phone numbers listed at the back of the book to make sure they were accurate. Checking 600 phone numbers is a pretty thankless job, but if that list proves useful to you, my wife deserves a big thank-you.

No project I am involved with could be completed without support from my colleagues at the *Boston Globe*. My boss, Peter Mancusi, encouraged this project and was confident enough in me that he never questioned the sleep-deprived look in my eyes or the many days I decided to work from home. Cheryl Appel, who edits my weekly columns, is a godsend, keeping both my spirits and the clarity of my writing up; she is a joy to work with.

In all of my work, my friend and mentor Ripley Hotch deserves some credit. He no longer edits my copy, but in our all-too-infrequent phone calls, he still inspires my self-confidence.

Obviously, this book owes heavily to the people I talk to each day, the best and brightest minds in the investment and money-management world. I have quoted a small number of these experts throughout the book, but they constantly shape my opinion and understanding of mutual funds and I am a whole lot smarter for my association with them. Suffice it to say, there are thousands of interviews from my years in journalism that are rolled into this book.

Lastly, I owe a special debt to the people who let me into their homes each week when they devote a few minutes to my columns. I don't know them by name, but in my mind's eye, they have become my friends, neighbors, and the muse for this whole undertaking. I get hundreds of letters and e-mails each week (far too many of which I can't get around to answering quickly); those notes from people just like you inspired this book and serve as a constant reminder that this book is necessary and useful, even in a world where fund information is only a phone call or mouse click away.

INTRODUCTION

A few years ago, I received a book that purported to list the 100 best mutual funds. The methodology for picking these winners was questionable, to put it kindly. It included a five-star system in which two stars were free (that's a three-star system trying to look important), and it did not include funds in several asset classes that many investors consider crucial, like virtually all types of bond funds.

The logic was flawed and there was no substance. The outcome was predictable: a list of funds that went on to produce mixed results. Yet the author told me that he was trying to throw investors a lifeline. With thousands of funds to choose from, he figured people were drowning in choices, and thus he would make things simple for them.

As I noted when I wrote about the book: "You can't save a drowning man by throwing him a cherry Lifesaver."

Reading what passes for personal finance advice these days spurred me to try to write something better. You will not find any insider's "secrets" or ways to beat the system here; that's not what mutual-fund investing is about. When it comes to funds, there are no secrets to owning good ones—solid research and proper planning are available for everyone who is willing to put in the time.

If you are looking for names of "the exact right funds to buy today," you can stop reading now. I can no more name the funds that are appropriate for you, an individual reader whose finances I know nothing about, than I can break the world weight-lifting record. The burden is just too heavy.

This book is not about doing the impossible; it's about the reality that you as a mutual-fund investor face, whether you are a novice or an expert. When it comes to charting a course for your financial future, you have decisions to make. You need to decide *what to buy, what to sell,* and *what to hold.*

This book will examine these issues and many others in detail. It will help you establish a framework that makes buying choices straightforward; it will help you determine the right time to jettison a fund; and best of all, it will help you with everything that comes in between.

You spend the vast majority of your time as an *owner* of funds, not as an active buyer or seller. But that doesn't mean that there won't be some tough challenges ahead. You'll experience speed bumps, for example, when a fund manager is replaced, or when fund performance is spotty, and also when your own needs or risk tolerance changes. This book covers those situations and also tries to help you develop a personal system to handle every eventuality of fund ownership, from first inquiry to getting your redemption check.

The book encourages you to think like an owner of funds, not as merely a buyer or end user. Too often, investors see themselves as being *along for the ride,* as if they have absolutely no power in the decisionmaking. That's very far from the truth. It's not as if you are buying soap or spaghetti and have to be content with what comes out of the box.

As an owner, you should question a fund's results, its policies and strategies. You are allowed to be upset when costs are too high and profits too low. You might not be able to effect change in the way the fund is managed, but you can make changes to your own portfolio any time you feel the need. In other words, you have power to control your mutual funds as long as you choose to exercise it. Likewise, you should exercise control in how you read this book, as it may not be necessary for you to read every section right now, from cover to cover. In fact, I think this book may be most useful if you concentrate on the parts that are most relevant to you today—and come back to the book again when your circumstances change and you need to handle a new situation that has arisen in your portfolio. If you just received a proxy statement from a fund, for example, you may need to read up on what to look for. That, in turn, might prompt you to seek information from the fund's prospectus, statement of additional information, and more. Following this introduction is a user's guide, which suggests how you might read this book depending on your circumstances.

I encourage you to go where the information takes you. In that way, you can use this book to learn or to refresh your memory. There will be no cherry Life-savers, no list of hot funds, and nothing that purports to do a job that you must do for yourself. Nor is this book a textbook that covers, say, technical analysis; if you want chapter and verse on something esoteric such as beta, you'll get an explanation (see page 130), but it won't be a detailed scholarly dissertation.

Instead, what you will find is everything you need to spend the rest of your life making money in mutual funds—all of the essentials that will allow you, on your own or with guidance, to do the job of buying, owning, and selling funds.

That job is not picking the hot funds of the moment but rather picking the best funds for *you* and assembling and managing a mutual-fund portfolio that enables you to reach your goals.

It won't be easy, but I guarantee it will be very worth your effort.

Now let's get to work.

A USER'S GUIDE
TO THIS BOOK

This book is designed to allow you to navigate according to your own prior knowledge. Unless you are an investor with no experience in funds, you are likely to find at least some information that you already know. Therefore, you have the option of skipping around, filling in knowledge based on your current situation. Then, over time, you can refer back to sections that are more applicable according to your current circumstances. In this way, the book functions very much like the owner's manual it is designed to be.

Of course, a less-experienced investor might choose to read this book from cover to cover in order to learn everything there is to know about mutual funds.

Listed below are common situations that fund investors face and a suggested reading list of sections that apply.

If you are a first-time fund investor or are expecting to buy funds outside of a 401(k) plan for the first time:
> *Must-read sections:* 2, 3, 4, 5, 6, 7, 8, 12, 15, 16, 22, 23, 24, 34
> *Recommended reading:* 9, 10, 13, 14, 25, 26, 31, 33, 35, 37

If you are hoping to expand a small portfolio:
> *Must-read sections:* 7, 8, 9, 11, 25, 26
> *Recommended reading:* 3, 4, 5, 6, 11, 13, 14, 15, 16, 19, 27, 28

If you are wondering whether your portfolio is on track for success:
> *Must-read sections:* 22, 23, 24, 25, 26, 27, 28, 29, 31, 37, 38

Recommended reading: 5, 6, 13, 14, 15, 38, 40

If you are concerned that your portfolio is out of control:
  Must-read sections: 24, 25, 26, 27, 37, 39, 40, 41
  Recommended reading: 5, 6, 23, 30, 35

If you are considering dumping funds that have disappointed you:
  Must-read sections: 5, 6, 25, 26, 27, 37, 39, 40, 43
  Recommended reading: 24, 38, 41, 42

If you have more than fifteen funds, including those in your retirement plans:
  Must-read sections: 25, 26, 27, 30, 35, 39
  Recommended reading: 20, 37, 39, 41

If you work with a financial adviser but want to take on more control of your affairs:
  Must-read sections: 3, 4, 5, 6, 7, 8, 11, 12, 13, 15, 30
  Recommended reading: 23, 24, 25, 26, 27, 28, 29, 35, 39

If you are fed up with "bad luck" picking funds:
  Must-read sections: 3, 4, 5, 6, 11, 13, 14, 15, 16, 19, 21, 24, 39
  Recommended reading: 8, 9, 26, 27, 37, 38, 40, 41, 42

If you are just looking to add one fund to your portfolio:
  Must-read sections: 4, 7, 8, 9, 10, 11, 25, 26
  Recommended reading: 5, 6, 13, 14, 15, 16, 21, 27, 28, 39

If you are looking for a shortcut through all of these other shortcuts:
  Must-read sections: The "furniture" segments at the end of each section, including "The Right Way to Proceed," "Something to Consider," "Wrong-Way Signs," "The Least You Should Remember," and other quick-hit advisories.

If you are wondering whether a section is worth your time, given your knowledge of the subject, skip right to the end. If you see yourself in the "wrong-way signs" or don't know the "least you should remember" or don't realize the "right way to proceed," then perhaps you should read that part of the book in its entirety.

PART ONE

WHEN YOU BUY

1
section

WHAT IS
A MUTUAL FUND?

IN THE FIRST SIXTY YEARS OF MUTUAL-FUND HISTORY, a book like this wasn't necessary because all funds did exactly the same thing: They turned your money over to a professional manager who ran it however he saw fit. The investment objective was always the same: to make you more money than you could get from a bank, and do it in relative safety. There was no asset allocation choice to make, no reason to own several funds, no real way to analyze the fund's performance against its peers, and no chance to look inside its portfolio.

Fund investing was a leap of faith. You trusted in the manager.

> Mutual funds remain a cost-effective way for any investor to achieve a diversified portfolio of stocks and bonds.

But fund investing was also something more. It was a way for the average person—one with neither great wealth nor market savvy—to get into the stock market. That hasn't changed in the fund industry's seventy-five-plus years.

What *has* changed, however, is the leeway that each fund manager has to choose investments. As the fund industry developed and matured, investors and financial advisers realized that there were ways to decrease the blind-faith factor and increase the science—mixing the right elements, then, to develop a portfolio and strategy.

Thanks to asset allocation, picking a superstar fund is less important than choosing a good long-term investment strategy. Virtually everyone in the fund world agrees that asset allocation—the way you divide your money among domestic and international stocks and bonds—will determine your earnings at least as surely as owning five funds that rank near the top of the near-term performance charts.

> More on asset allocation in Section 25.

Underlying it all, however, mutual funds are fairly simple investment vehicles that have not changed much structurally over the years. Technically speaking, a mutual fund is a pool of money, and each investor who joins in has a stake in the assets of the fund and shares proportionally in the gains or losses. So, if a fund has $100 million in assets and you have $10,000 invested, you own 0.01 percent of that fund. If the stocks that the fund owns were to double in value tomorrow, the fund would have $200 million in assets, and your stake would be worth $20,000.

Each fund chooses to purchase stocks or bonds, or both, in accordance with its "investment objective." A fund's investment objective, described in greater detail in Section 7, is essentially a stated goal concerning what the fund wants to achieve and how it plans to achieve it. These perfunctory descriptions tend to be pretty vague, for example: *The fund invests in growth companies that provide long-term capital appreciation.*

> The number of stocks and bonds each fund buys also varies widely. Some buy thousands of stocks, others as few as fifteen or twenty.

Each fund also has an "investment style" that it adheres to—value investing, global investing, growth investing, and so on—meaning it buys stocks of a certain size or bearing certain common financial traits. Each share you own in a fund is actually a tiny sliver of all of the fund's stocks, and the value of one of your shares is equal to the total worth of stocks or bonds in the fund's portfolio, divided by the number of shares outstanding.

Unlike an individual stock, which can trade up or down based on the sentiment of the market toward a company or industry, fund prices are entirely objective, reflecting only what the market says each fund share is worth. Your share in a fund entitles you to a piece of gains, losses, and taxes experienced by the fund. You also share in the fund's expenses, most notably the fee charged by management for handling the money.

For decades, most fund investors paid little attention to the taxes and expenses attached to their funds, therefore overlooking key factors in the size of their profits and their ability to share in the gains of the stock market. Today, smart investors include a fund's tax efficiency and expenses in their planning process.

> Mutual-fund fees, taxes, and expenses are described in detail in Sections 13, 19, and 31.

In today's mutual-fund environment, the name of the game is building a portfolio. To do that, you must have a very clear understanding of how a specific fund is investing. In the old days, now anything before the early 1990s, managers were allowed to take funds in whatever direction they pleased. Peter Lynch, the legendary manager of Fidelity Magellan, for example, once moved his fund into bonds because he believed that's where he could best manage his money at the time. But when Jeff Vinik, one of Lynch's successors at Magellan, did the same thing in the mid-1990s, it cost him his job. Investors fled the fund, saying a *stock* fund should not make market-timing decisions or concentrate in bonds. The whole fund industry noticed.

As the public demanded more accountability from funds and more accuracy in investment objectives, funds became more highly specialized. So, an investor who wants to cover the whole spectrum of the stock market can do that either with one very broad fund or, more likely, with several funds dedicated to specific market areas. Fund managers pick stocks in certain defined segments of the market, leaving the bigger portfolio decisions—percentage into large stocks, percentage into bonds, and so forth—to individual investors.

> Today, most individual investors wisely choose to spread their money out over various asset classes, investing with several separate funds rather than having one fund manager decide when it's a good time to own stocks versus bonds.

And that's why a book like this one is necessary.

THE LEAST YOU SHOULD REMEMBER

As an individual investor, you have thousands of funds to choose from in dozens of different asset classes. But choosing and managing a portfolio of mutual funds usually comes down to focusing on a number of factors, notably: assets, expenses, track record, management style, risk and volatility, the role of a fund in your portfolio, tax efficiency, and the ability to develop the conviction to take the plunge with confidence.

It is in examining these key factors that you can distinguish one fund from another and determine which ones are worth owning.

> *An investor cannot earn superior profits from stocks simply by committing to a specific category or style. He can earn them by carefully evaluating facts and continuously exercising discipline.*
>
> —WARREN BUFFETT,
> CHAIRMAN OF BERKSHIRE HATHAWAY CORPORATION

2

WHY MUTUAL FUNDS?

IT MIGHT SEEM THAT EVERYONE OWNS MUTUAL FUNDS these days, but the truth is that no one actually needs to. You can get everything a mutual fund delivers by investing in individual stocks. In fact, there are all kinds of web sites, on-line communities and clubs that will tell you that funds are passé. They argue that funds have high costs—relative to buying stocks through a discount broker—and that actively managed funds frequently don't beat the index they are measured against. Typically, the anti-fund arguments claim that you might be able to beat the market by building your own stock portfolio, possibly by using an index fund to give you broad stock market exposure and then selecting the right stocks to own around it.

Index funds are described in detail in Section 9.

In short, these arguments are absolutely correct. You can buy stocks on your own in a cost-effective manner. And you might also be able to outperform the stock market with a few well-placed picks. But to develop your own investment portfolio without using funds, you are going to need to allocate both time and money. You will need to do your own research—enough to feel comfortable developing and implementing a diversified investment strategy—or you will need the resources to hire someone to do it for you. And if you have to pay someone to

Even if you generally shy away from funds, you are likely to have them in your retirement plan or 401(k).

build your stock portfolio, chances are that you will not have any cost advantages over mutual funds.

Mutual funds, therefore, are a necessity for some people and a convenience for many others. But in all cases, they are a way to accomplish several financial goals with one purchase. And that is part of why they can be so tricky to choose and manage.

> With mutual funds, diversification and professional management come at a relatively low cost.

It is much easier to select one stock than to choose one mutual fund. With a stock, you are looking for good numbers, coupled with a good investment story and a market outlook that makes sense. With a fund, however, you are trying to determine what the manager will do, what kinds of stocks fit into the portfolio, whether the fund's objectives match your own, and how it all fits together in one package.

That said, it remains much easier to choose a single diversified mutual fund than to build and manage a portfolio of stocks. Building a stock portfolio requires that you understand how each one fits the portfolio and how they combine to give you diversification across various industries and sectors. That's what the anti-fund crowd forgets. Stock picking just isn't as easy as it seems.

Even if you've made a few great calls, you have probably also selected a few dogs that you would prefer to forget. Your overall performance is inclusive, however, which is why funds have a place in a portfolio as an adjunct to or in place of individual stocks.

The reasons for owning funds are simple and are covered below.

> Although buying one stock is easier than purchasing one mutual fund, building a portfolio of stocks is much more complicated than putting together a portfolio of funds.

DIVERSIFICATION

Although there are "nondiversified" funds, the vast majority of offerings spread your assets over a wide range of stocks. The Securities and Exchange Commission (SEC) mandates that a fund cannot have more than 5 percent of its assets in any one stock and still be considered "diversified." Complicating matters, that rule actually applies to only three-fourths of a fund's holdings, meaning the fund could actually have 25 percent of its assets in one stock and then no more than 5 percent of the rest in any other stock. Therefore, a diversified portfolio holds at least sixteen different issues (5 percent times fifteen issues equals 75 percent of the portfolio, plus the one holding that can grow to as much as 25 percent). But most funds hold far more stocks than that, and some of the largest funds hold hundreds or thousands of individual stocks.

Most financial advisers say that individuals trying to build their own stock portfolio would need at least fifteen issues to consider their holdings diversified. That's where the time factor comes in; managing that many stocks on your own—particularly if you periodically trade stocks that fall out of favor—is not easy.

Diversification also tends to stabilize performance. Holding only one stock is an all-eggs-in-one-basket approach to investing. Good times look very good, but hard times can look mighty desperate. The more stocks you have, the more you spread that risk and increase the chance that at least some of your holdings will be moving in the right direction at all times. Funds, by comparison, represent a many-eggs-in-many-baskets approach.

> It is entirely possible to build a diversified investment portfolio by purchasing just a few funds.

Funds are also an easy way to cover vast parts of the market that you might otherwise miss. Even if you are a dedicated stock investor, chances are you can only keep tabs on certain segments of the market. Funds can cover many different investment arenas, from all types of domestic bonds to international stocks, from large-company to small-cap stocks, and everything in between. The idea for a fund investor, therefore, is to assemble a diversified portfolio that includes a few funds that cover different areas of the market. For a stock investor, funds fill in the gaps. In either case, funds allow for broad market exposure and the ability to put together a portfolio that diversifies the risk into various types of global assets.

PROFESSIONAL MANAGEMENT

Try to think of your money in the same way you would any other valuable asset—your car, for example. If you have the expertise to change the oil and do your own repairs, that's great. If not, you need to hire someone to make sure that your car keeps rolling in the right direction. Fund managers are, in this case, financial mechanics. You hire them to tackle the work you aren't willing or able to do yourself.

No matter what style of investing you subscribe to, there are mutual-fund managers out there who engage in that approach. Regardless of whether you want to invest exclusively in high-growth companies, Internet stocks, environmentally friendly businesses, or, if you are looking for bargains, domestic or international companies, some or several existing funds will serve your needs.

> The right professional management is an important selling point for mutual funds; the tricky part is knowing how to assess what a specific fund manager does. See Section 9 for details.

BUYING POWER

Building a portfolio of individual stocks can tie up a big chunk of money. Most funds, however, have reasonable minimums of no more than a few thousand dollars, and many fund families waive those initial requirements for anyone who signs up to make small, automatic monthly deposits. Pooling money in a fund allows investors who aren't rich to afford professional management and can provide diversification that they could not assemble on their own.

CONVENIENCE

There is a lot to be said for the ease of maintenance provided by mutual funds. For most investors, this means incorporating a buy-and-hold strategy and combining it with a simple review process every few months. What's more, investors can make systematic deposits or withdrawals into funds, allowing for easy dollar-cost averaging. Many funds even allow for electronic direct deposit from a customer's paycheck.

> Dollar-cost averaging is a strategy of buying fund shares by investing the same amount of additional money on a regular schedule, usually monthly, to maximize buying power and minimize volatility.

Individual stocks are a more complicated and expensive purchase because you need to amass enough cash to make a cost-effective trade. On the sales side, funds and stocks are about equal; both usually can be sold with nothing more than a phone call.

OWNERSHIP

The key with funds is to remember that you are an owner. All too often, investors—and investment companies—treat funds like "product," something to "buy" rather than something to "own."

With stocks, the feeling of ownership is present because of proxy votes and statements and because investors read the breaking financial news about their favorite stocks. Funds, by comparison, typically don't make news, and most function without shareholder meetings.

But this doesn't mean that the ownership element of mutual funds is unimportant. In fact, it's crucial. As an owner, you are an active partner—you are in charge of the investment and you control its place in your overall portfolio.

THE RIGHT WAY TO PROCEED

Start by deciding how much of your money belongs in mutual funds versus other investments. Then, look at your investments as a unit and use funds to fill in areas where they are deficient. If you own individual stocks or bonds, your mutual funds should complement those holdings. If you are strictly a fund investor, each fund in your portfolio should complement the others. The result, in both cases, will be an investment portfolio that delivers the benefits of diversification.

SEVEN STEPS TO BUYING A FUND

WHEN MUTUAL FUNDS WERE FIRST CREATED IN THE 1920S, there wasn't much skill involved in picking the right one. For starters, the entire universe of funds could be counted on both hands. Secondly, all of those funds did the same thing.

Today, with more than 10,000 mutual funds investing in more ways than the people who created the business could ever have imagined, the selection process is a bit more complicated.

But it's not as complicated as passing the Series 6 stockbroker exam.

> The key to building a good portfolio is developing a methodology for choosing a fund and then sticking with it.

SEVEN IMPORTANT STEPS

Most investors can develop personalized fund-picking criteria that will leave them with sound choices by following the seven steps outlined below. Although individual goals might necessitate placing greater importance on one element or another, each factor is a weigh station on the road to buying a fund.

Keep in mind that the steps below are presented in overview format. Important components of each are described in more detail in the sections that follow.

1. Determine why you want or need a new fund. Investing is both a passage to a better future and a hobby. Never confuse the two. This means avoiding impulse buying and moves that don't fit into a larger strategy. The process of picking a fund differs from individual to individual—and starts when you decide what you want your money to accomplish. Setting your goals and expectations involves sorting out which types of funds you should consider and deciding whether you really need a new fund at all or whether adding to existing holdings would be sufficient.

> Before purchasing mutual funds you must determine your individual investment objective. See Section 7 for more details.

2. Choose funds that meet both your needs and desires. If you're in the market for a new fund, you can quickly narrow the field of candidates by sticking to those that fit into your overall investment needs and limiting your choices to the specific asset classes you are interested in.

Many investors make the mistake of looking at performance numbers first, which then causes them to purchase the same type of funds over and over, resulting in a portfolio that has a lot of similar funds but little diversification. Four of a kind may be a winning poker hand, but holding four of the same type of mutual funds can suck the life out of each individual fund's performance.

> Specific asset classes represented by mutual funds include: large-cap growth, small-cap value, bonds, and international stocks. See Section 8 for more details.

Aside from asset class, look for basic characteristics that are important to you. If you are buying funds without the assistance of a financial adviser, for example, you probably want to consider only the no-load variety—funds without a sales charge. Features like check writing might be important to you, or you might want to stay within one fund family or fund supermarket in order to ease the weight in your mailbox each month.

> See Section 12 for more information on load versus no-load funds.

Another factor to consider is financial commitment. Some funds may require a minimum initial investment that is beyond your means. Don't waste your time pining away for those funds. Find out if they waive minimums for people who agree to invest money automatically each month; or simply move on.

See Section 13 for more information on expenses.

This initial process of elimination will leave you with a pared-down list of funds to choose from. To shrink the list further, wipe out funds with above-average expenses or below-average performance over the last few years. The result of this exercise is likely to leave you with a workable list of names from which you can find one or two finalists.

3. Learn the history of the fund or its manager. Fund investing is a leap of faith. You need something tangible to base that faith on, whether it is the expertise of an investment genius or the consistency of a specific style of investing such as indexing. Either way, look for a compelling reason to go with a particular fund, something that will give you the will to stay invested during choppy markets.

You can often find that motivation in the fund's newsletters—where the best managers in the business tell you a lot about their style and discipline in the information they provide for shareholders and prospective investors. Call the funds you are most interested in and ask for recent letters to shareholders (virtually all will send them along with a prospectus). The fund may also provide recent fund reviews or other media pieces. Consider the source of such information carefully; if it does not come from a writer, data service, or publication you know and respect—or if it is based on some selection criteria that are not fully explained—dig deeper on your own.

4. Examine performance, particularly over the long term. Most people start the process here, but the stock market joyride of the 1990s has actually made return data less meaningful. Look at returns from the vantage points of consistency and satisfactory percentages relative to peers. You most likely will not want a fund with below-average results compared to its peers—I look for funds in the top 25 percent of their peer group—and you may not be able to stick with a fund that is prone to volatile swings, even if it tops the charts often enough to have a good long-term record.

Study the fund's worst quarter and project those losses out over a full year to give yourself an idea of what might happen if the investment climate gets scary. Turn the bar charts in the prospectus upside down; any fund capable of earning 40 percent in a year is equally capable of losing that much. Be sure you have an idea of how bumpy things could get before you strap yourself in for a wild ride.

> It's vital to read and understand a fund's prospectus. See Section 34 for details.

And before checking off on performance, look at recent data from a ratings service like Morningstar or Value Line to give you independent verification that you haven't fallen for sweetheart numbers. In 1999, for example, several growth funds advertised average annual gains of more than 15 percent for the preceding five years. That looks great on paper until you realize that they trailed the leading growth funds by more than 2 percent per year and lagged the Standard & Poor's 500 Index, too.

5. **Choose the finalists and call for three to five prospectuses.**   Don't hone in on one fund before you call for the paperwork. You will want to make sure a fund's holdings are consistent with the manager's discipline and need to understand what the fund is allowed to invest in, which is a key to how the portfolio could change in the future.

> Always look past the raw data for some measure of relative performance.

Be sure you understand the written materials the fund provides. Unfortunately, many fund companies write all of their documents in what seems like "fundspeak," rather than English (even though the SEC has tried hard to change that). Calling for the prospectuses tells you a lot about a fund company. If they don't jump at the chance to answer questions before you have an account, you can expect similarly disappointing treatment once you sign on as a customer.

6. **Look at expense ratios and turnover.**   This is a great way to weed out your short list. A fund is entitled to its cut, but higher-than-average expenses are unnecessary. Funds with low turnover rates, meanwhile, tend to be tax- and cost-efficient. You are looking for funds that can be trusted in all market conditions. In a sour market, funds with the big expense ratios and high turnover are likely to suffer more than the rest.

7. Write down the reasons you are buying the fund, then write the check.
Start and maintain a file for any new investment you own. The first thing in that file should be a list of all the reasons you are choosing a specific fund. The list should include where you heard about the fund and what initially attracted you, expectations for annual returns or performance compared to peers, what the fund is supposed to be adding to your portfolio, supporting factors that influenced your decision (such as star ratings), concerns you have about the fund, and anything else that has entered into your decision.

> Turnover refers to how often a manager buys and sells the stocks that make up the fund portfolio. See Section 14 for more details.

This will come in handy later when you try to measure whether a fund has lived up to your expectations. Say, for example, that your key considerations in picking a small-company stock fund were: a five-star rating from Morningstar, performance in the top quarter of its peer group, and below-average expense ratio. If five years from now the fund has underperformed its peers and lost its great rating—or if you have purchased another fund that gives you small-cap exposure with better performance—you will see that some of your crucial decision points no longer exist and that you may want to make a change.

When you finish writing this list of reasons to buy the fund, you're ready to write the check. If you can't pull the trigger after this initial preparation, something is wrong. If you're feeling hesitant about buying a particular fund or funds, don't go through with the transaction. Go back and start this seven-step process over again.

THE LEAST YOU SHOULD REMEMBER

Investing is about reaching goals, not beating markets. If you focus the process on your investment objectives, you are more likely to be happy with your selection than if you focus strictly on performance and independent ratings.

TWELVE QUESTIONS TO ASK BEFORE YOU BUY

THERE ARE THOUSANDS OF GROWTH STOCK FUNDS but only eight to ten ways to actually manage one. Likewise, there are only a few questions investors really *must* answer in order to cut those thousands of funds down to the few that will best meet their needs.

Having already examined the big-picture issues, it's time to turn to the specific questions most investors should ask and answer before buying a fund. Essentially, in taking those seven steps toward buying a fund, a dozen questions will help you determine if a fund is a good match for your personality and portfolio.

Your preinvestment questions actually have more to do with you than the fund you are considering. As Morningstar, Inc. president Don Phillips puts it: "The questions about yourself are the ones you can answer with the most degree of certainty, so getting those answers first is probably the biggest factor in being satisfied with the fund you buy."

TWELVE CRITICAL PREINVESTMENT QUESTIONS

1. What do I want to achieve with this money, and what types of funds meet that goal? There are myriad reasons to invest—funding education, retirement, or a home—but they boil down to a few characteristics you want from an investment. Generally, personal investment objectives are safety, current income, long-term growth, or a balance of all three.

> If you choose a fund before determining your investment goals, you are relying more on luck than strategy.

By isolating the investment purpose—say you need short-term growth in order to buy a house soon—you can start searching for funds that meet your goal. If you buy the fund before deciding what the money is for, when you will need it, and how much you need it to grow, you could wind up with an investment that is too risky or volatile or too conservative for your purposes.

2. What is my time horizon for this investment?   How much do I have to invest over that time?   The time you have to achieve goals is an important factor in determining the risks you can take and the appropriate assets to buy. Typically, a longer time frame makes you more aggressive. You know better than anyone else when a tuition payment is due, when the car will need to be replaced, and when you plan to retire.

Another factor driving the decision is how much you have to invest and how much you need to reach a specified goal. If, for example, a child is ten years away from college but you already have the tuition money saved, you may opt to avoid the market and pick ultrasafe investments in order to avoid the potential for the market to eat up the principal.

> Money you need in less than two years (or less than five years if you consider yourself a conservative investor) should probably not be exposed to the stock market at all.

Conversely, if you don't have enough saved yet, you may decide to put the money into more aggressive investment vehicles, hoping to catch up. How much you need to gain and how much you can afford to lose should always be in the back of your mind as you decide which types of funds are right for you.

3. How much risk can I live with?   This is the toughest question of all, because most people are quick to say that they can tolerate any risk—"so long as I don't lose money."

It doesn't work that way.

The financial services world looks at risk and volatility in complicated mathematical terms like beta, alpha, and standard deviation. Individual investors need to look at risk in terms of dollars and cents. Try to picture yourself in the fund during a down market. If funds you are considering weren't around for downturns, use the average performance of the asset group during market doldrums.

> Beta, alpha, and standard deviation are explained in Section 21.

Think, too, about the mathematics of volatility. If a fund goes up 50 percent one year, then down 50 percent the next—the way it looks on a bar chart—you might think the fund broke even. But that's not real math. A $10,000 investment in the fund finished the first year worth $15,000, but the 50-percent loss dropped it to $7,500. The fund may look even, but you don't come out that way.

The stock market tends to reward long-term investors, and there is good reason to believe that an above-average fund will be able to recover from a market downturn if you give it time. That's why it's important to determine up front if you will be able to withstand the volatility and give the fund time without selling in a panic.

> If that fund-at-its-worst feeling makes you ill—regardless of the fund's upside potential—you need less risk.

4. Does this investment diversify my portfolio and fit my asset allocation plan?   Diversification—buying different kinds of assets and thereby reducing the overall risk of your investment portfolio—is the investment world's free lunch. It comes along with each new fund you buy, provided you are spreading your assets around into multiple asset classes.

If a new investment does not diversify the portfolio, you have a few choices: (1) drop the fund in favor of something in an asset class you don't currently own; (2) buy it anyway, knowing that funds with a lot of overlap don't actually diversify the portfolio; (3) buy the fund and sell the one you have now that covers the same area; (4) consider adding the money to a fund you already own instead.

> Asset allocation and diversification are explained in detail in Sections 25 and 26.

If choices 2, 3, and 4 seem too risky or make your portfolio too concentrated, then you need to change your asset allocation. The best way to do that is by investing in a fund that holds assets different from the funds you own now.

5. What are my alternatives?   Smart investors always consider what else is out there. If you could be satisfied with a no-risk return of 5 percent, chances are your money belongs in Treasury bills. Conversely, if you have laid the foundation for your portfolio and want to pursue some higher risk or higher growth investing, you might be considering individual stocks compared to, say, sector funds.

> Types of funds from growth funds to bond funds to sector funds are presented in Section 8.

Just because the world seems obsessed with funds does not mean you need to be. Always examine your other options; it's the best way to feel comfortable with whatever you invest in. In addition, remember that you may already hold the alternatives. As noted, one alternative to any new fund is simply buying additional shares of funds you already own. If you hold more than five funds, this may be a particularly viable option.

6. Do I have a special criterion for selecting a fund?   Social investors, for example, want funds invested in companies that adhere to particular social, moral, or ethical standards. No-load investors do not want to pay sales fees (and may opt against any funds charging annual marketing fees). Low-cost investors want funds with below-average expense ratios.

Some investors like to find small "undiscovered" funds, others like to invest with companies that have names they know. You might be involved in a mutual-fund supermarket program and might prefer to limit your choices to funds available in the program.

Be honest about your personal agenda. If you want to follow an investment theme, consider mostly funds that fit into it. If you ignore these personal criteria to invest in a fund with fancy performance numbers, you are likely to be unhappy with your selection down the road. Performance fades, but personal feelings do not. If or when returns start to slide on a fund that does not meet your personal agenda, you are very likely to change your portfolio again in order to get something in keeping with your values. Avoid that by acknowledging your preferences in advance.

7. Do I understand the data I'm looking at?   Morningstar, Inc., for example, gives a risk-reward rating of up to five stars. *Mutual Funds* magazine grades funds on its own five-star scale. So, too, do several books on "good funds to buy now." Some newsletters do forecasts involving expected returns; others forecast by giving each fund a letter grade.

The vagaries of each system make it possible for poor choices—based on your personal criteria—to earn high grades. Funds themselves contribute to this confusion. Some measure performance against the stock market but offer no indication of how the fund did relative to its peers. Without that relative performance, you have no clear idea of the fund's potential and whether it is worth taking a chance on.

Other funds determine their record using slippery time periods, omitting or blurring times when they did not look so good. If they had strong performance a few years ago, for example, they may show long track records that cover up their recent doldrums. And if the immediate past has been good, their ads won't show long-term records anywhere but in the fine print.

In the fall of 1999, for example, the Al Frank Fund sent out a notice that its most recent one-year performance, for the twelve-month period ending September 30, 1999, was a chart-topping gain of 47 percent. But the fine print on the notice told a different story. It showed that the fund's gain since inception—a period of twenty-one months starting just three quarters prior to the big-win year—was an annualized gain of 7 percent. In short, the fund had been a money loser before going gangbusters.

To be a confident investor, you must be comfortable with the data used to make your decision.

8. What is the fund's performance potential?   Most people make past performance the big factor in choosing a fund but mistakenly examine performance only in lump-sum terms. They see a fund with great three-year numbers and don't look past the annualized average return to find out what really happened.

Two funds could claim a 20-percent annualized average return and both be accurate. But one fund could achieve that result with three straight years of 20-percent gains, whereas another goes up 100 percent one year, down 15 percent the second, and then is flat during the third year.

> Section 15 discusses what past performance really says about a fund.

As noted, big gains cover a multitude of performance sins, allowing funds to stay atop the long-term charts even when returns are no longer terrific. Therefore, it's crucial for an investor to gauge performance by looking at it in three ways: annualized gains, year-by-year returns, and returns relative to the appropriate index and fund group.

You will find a line in every prospectus that says "past performance is no guarantee of future results." This means that you can't count on a fund providing the same kind of returns it has in the past. But regardless of that, you can look to see if a fund has been able to consistently deliver respectable numbers and beat its peers. Look first, therefore, at the appropriate benchmark or index, which gives you an idea of how the fund's assets perform over time. If you are buying a small-company growth fund, for example, the Russell 2000 Index will give you a picture of how small stocks have done over the long haul. You can expect your long-term return to be similar to what the asset group gets as a whole.

Because so many funds were created in the 1990s, when downturns were few and far between, the yearly graphs may not show you how the fund might perform in a bear market. For that, turn the performance chart upside down or put a minus sign in front of the fund's best year.

Look next at annualized gains against both the index and the fund's peer group, usually measured by a Lipper Index. This lets you see how performance stacks up. The more consistent the performance pattern against peers and index, the easier it is to determine whether the fund is worthy. Obviously, you are looking for the ability to meet or exceed the average fund over time; if a fund has been able to do that for several years running, it is showing signs that it can deliver consistently.

Look last at year-by-year returns. This is mostly to see how smooth the ride has been for shareholders and whether the fund has been steady or volatile.

No one complains about volatility on the upside, when a fund is up by 40 percent. But any fund that can gain that much in a year could lose that much, too, so be sure you examine the fund's yearly volatility, picture a worst-case scenario, and are certain you could stay put through the darkest of times. If the prospect of the fund's best year going negative against you is too frightening to sit through, you need to find another fund.

Ultimately, most investors want consistently superior performance, something that is above average but not topping the charts (because funds that reach the very top of the performance list often turn around and hit the bottom of those same lists periodically). Look for return numbers that convince you that the fund you are about to buy will stand the test of time.

9. What am I willing to pay to get that performance? This is both about applicable sales charges and loads, as well as ongoing expenses.

Sales charges boil down to a simple question: Is this fund worth the amount that I am paying my financial adviser for selecting it for me? Is there another option that is just as good, with a lower charge?

Typically, the answer boils down to your need for a financial adviser at all. If all you want is someone to choose funds for you, you most likely will find that no sales charge is ever worth it. If you need a financial adviser for bigger, broader advice on how to manage your money, reasonable fees are fair.

When it comes to ongoing expenses, everything is relative. In a year when the market is up 35 percent, a 2.5-percent expense ratio doesn't look bad. But in the future, when the market earns just 5 percent, half of your profits will go straight to the fund. And in a flat year, you will post a loss just so you can pay the fund's management. The average stock mutual fund charges anywhere from 1.25 percent to 1.5 percent for expenses. By comparison, an index fund may charge less than 0.2 percent (which is why index funds are considered a low-cost alternative).

In bond funds, average expenses are lower, closer to 1 percent, but matter even more. Simply put, there are not many ways to manage a bond fund and make it unique; because of that, studies show that higher costs almost invariably lead to lower long-term returns.

> Costs matter, from fees to expense ratios. You may choose to ignore them in good times, but don't be caught unawares. If you pay too much for a fund, it is almost certain to bother you sometime in the future.

In either stock or bond funds, you want to make sure that the manager has the ability to invest in the way you want—a style you like and agree with and need to add to your portfolio—at a reasonable cost.

Even if performance is terrific, don't discount a big expense ratio. Arguably the worst funds in history, the Steadman Funds, had expense ratios of more than 10 percent, yet they periodically would have a great quarter or six months. Over time, however, the true color of the funds emerged; they simply could not sustain performance that could overcome the anchor of high expenses.

10. Who manages the fund, how long has that person been there, and what happens when that person leaves? Performance is a direct reflection of choices made by the fund manager. If the fund has a successful history but the current manager was not responsible for its good times, it should make you nervous. If the manager has a long record of running the fund smoothly, that should increase your confidence.

As the fund industry has evolved, specific managers have become less important than the style of assets a fund buys. Still, you want to have some comfort level that the person handling your money can actually do the job you are hiring a fund manager for. Likewise, if you plan to be a buy-and-hold investor, you may someday have to worry about the fund's ability to replace the manager.

In the summer of 1999, for example, manager Ryan Jacob left The Internet Fund to start his own firm. The Internet Fund's performance suffered thereafter, and while it is hard to determine whether it was the absence of Jacob or a decline among Internet stocks that caused the falloff, the change in management coupled with declining performance was enough to shake some investors.

By comparison, Jim Craig, the star manager of the Janus Fund, announced in the fall of 1999 that he would turn the fund over to an associate. Because Janus has a history of replacing talented managers from within and for making those changes without compromising the long-term record of the funds involved—and because Craig was going to stay with the company as director of research—few investors got worried.

Determine what might happen to the fund if the manager left. The big fund firms typically have a deep bench and can bring someone up from within. The small, eclectic, often eponymous fund companies may not have that luxury. If you want to own a fund for a lifetime, look for that deep bench, the talent that can replace a manager. It's okay if your current manager is the big star of the show, but it does mean that the fund will bear watching more closely if his or her situation changes.

11. Can I live by the rules of this fund? This actually involves several questions, ranging from whether you can afford the fund's minimum initial investment to whether you like how the fund handles transactions to whether you can do business on-line or by phone.

You might be used to a fund group with a twenty-four-hour phone service center and electronic transfer privileges, but some funds work business hours and require signature guarantees—a letter authenticating your John Hancock—before you can sell. Avoid trouble by learning a fund's rules up front.

12. What are the big selling points for this fund? What are the big negatives?
These are the last questions because they force you to review the entire process and focus on why you are adding this particular investment to your portfolio.

To avoid frustration, know the details of buying and selling shares, as well any transaction fees specific to the fund.

As noted in the last chapter, you will want to start your relationship with a fund by writing down all of the reasons you bought it, every factor that attracted you and had a hand in your decision, from what you wanted the fund to do to the performance factors you liked, and so on. In short, sell yourself on the fund one more time, and pay careful attention to any possible negatives. If the upside doesn't obliterate the negatives, it's probably time to scrap the fund and start the process over again.

If you have answered the first eleven questions, however, chances are that you will feel confident about the reasons a particular fund is worth adding to your portfolio.

WRONG-WAY SIGNS

If you put performance factors at the top of your selection criteria, everything else will fall apart because you are almost certain to wind up chasing hot funds, and you will become dissatisfied when they cool off.

Performance is important, but you need to remember that fund investing is not a competition. You want good, solid funds, but it is not important that you have the "number one fund" in a category. There's an old saying that every twenty-four hours, the world turns over on someone who was sitting atop it; nowhere is that more true than in the mutual-fund business.

THE RIGHT WAY TO PROCEED

Examine how you selected funds in the past, the steps you followed, and questions you asked. Based on this section, see if there is anything you missed that you might add to your current selection process. Look also for anything that you want from a fund that was not covered here.

Your personal selection method for a fund should reflect the factors you consider most important. The idea is to develop a discipline, a way of choosing funds that deliver results in keeping with your expectations. Since your expectations are personal, your method for picking funds might be highly personal too.

5

CHARACTERISTICS OF A WINNING FUND

EVERY DAY, ANOTHER TIME PERIOD PASSES, be it the most current week, twelve months, or five years. Every three months, the newest lists of winners are widely disseminated, so that investors can scour them to review performance and, perhaps, pick the next winner.

Look at enough performance charts, however, and you start to see common occurrences. On the short-term three-month and one-year charts, you find that winning funds tend to be in the right place, making big bets at just the time to get a big payoff. In addition, short-term winners are more aggressive—and hence more volatile—than their peers; that shoot-for-the-stars aggression can overcome high expense ratios and sales charges over short periods, sometimes making lousy funds look decent.

If you need proof that many funds atop the short-term charts are more lucky than good, look at the bottom of those charts. There you will find the same kind of high-risk, stylized funds that lack only in the fortuitous timing. They're bottom feeding, for now, not because management is inept but because their style or assets are out of step with the market. That could change in the next quarter or year, when their place in the market becomes the "right one" for the moment.

The common traits of funds on the long-term winners list are usually a little harder to spot—but they exist. Recognizing the following characteristics—and

> A fund that combines winning characteristics with the investment objectives that meet your needs will give you a pretty good shot at long-term satisfaction.

they hold true no matter what a fund invests in—makes it easier to pick a winner.

DISCIPLINE

Superior long-term funds stick to their guns, no matter what the market conditions are. Whether that discipline is purchasing undervalued stocks, identifying growth companies, or moving from sector to sector in an effort to remain one step ahead of the market, a manager who believes in the long-term viability of the strategy will not waver.

This is one of the keys to success with index investing. Since index funds are passively managed, they do not change strategies midstream, holding instead to the basket of stocks they are tied to. There is no emotion in the management process, so there is no chance that a portfolio manager will get scared and stray from what has worked in the past.

> Index funds are discussed in greater detail in Section 8.

Discipline holds true for most of the best active managers in any asset allocation, who typically do whatever they do best even when the market is working against them. Finding out whether a fund has discipline and sticks to it is hard to uncover in a prospectus. Although some managers come out and say specifically what they are looking for—stocks with a low price-to-earnings (P/E) ratio or a low price, stocks or sectors with growth potential greater than 10 percent per year, for example—most talk in generalities.

So ask the questions: What makes this fund buy something, and what makes it sell? The more specific the answer, the more you can judge the style; just as important, the easier it is to tell when the manager loses confidence and changes the style.

Years ago, the Monetta Fund was a highflier, thanks to some very strong buy and sell disciplines. Manager Bob Baccarella would sell his winners after they ran up gains of a certain size and sell before declines became too big. But the funds also benefited from some very good market calls, and when Baccarella got out of step with the market, performance started to fade. Once that happened, the funds broke discipline, with both winners and losers being held longer.

"You wound up with a manager who was chasing hot stuff in ways that really didn't make sense given that investors bought the fund because of its safe, steady approach," says Stephen M. Savage, editor of the *No-Load Fund Analyst* newsletter. "Once a manager breaks discipline and starts chasing things around, they may never catch up. Disciplined managers know that the market will come back to them."

BRAVERY TO GO AGAINST THE CROWD

Great funds are not necessarily contrarian by nature, but the discipline just discussed often leads to moves that look that way, such as continuing to favor the value style of investing when the market favors a more growth-oriented style.

What that means is consistent winners sometimes look a little crazy in the eyes of the market. John Neff, the legendary former manager of the Vanguard Windsor Fund, for example, was routinely early in his market assessments; he saw things before the competition, and he moved on what he saw. That meant that there were times when the stocks he owned were dogs and his short-term performance suffered. Neff didn't care, however, because he was confident his selections would be borne out over time. He usually was right.

> If a fund manager does not exhibit courage in his investment strategy, it becomes difficult to believe the fund will be a long-term winner.

CONSISTENCY

The ideal performance for a long-term winner is a ranking among the top 10 to 20 percent of its peers without having finished among the top or bottom ten funds in any single quarter. In baseball terms, these funds tend to be "singles hitters," seldom striking out and producing small gains consistently without ever smacking prodigious quarterly home runs.

To be a long-term winner, a fund needs only to beat its peers and benchmarks by a fraction over the short run. But consistency comes in many forms, including consistent volatility. A more volatile fund can be a long-term winner but must beat the market sufficiently on the upswing to look good after slogging through the bottoms. What's more, that ride is so bumpy that it's hard to stay in the fund long enough to benefit.

Take, for example, Kenneth Heebner of the CGM Funds, who is widely acknowledged as one of the best managers ever but who has been called the "Mad Bomber" for his style of making heavy, often contrarian bets on the market.

If you had invested with Heebner's CGM Capital Development Fund in 1979 and had then fallen into a twenty-year coma, you would have awakened pretty happy, with a gain of more than 3,900 percent, more than 20 percent annualized per year and more than double its average peer over that time. Had you been awake the whole time, however, you might not have made it through the twenty years. Despite the fact that Heebner spent five of those years as the top-gaining fund in his peer group and posted a 99-percent return in the fund in 1991, many shareholders thought he had "lost it" just three years later, when his fund lost almost 23 percent and was dead last among its peers.

Heebner certainly has discipline and the bravery to stick by his own convictions, but his form of consistency is that he sticks to a formula that has produced tremendous volatility. That's fine, so long as you recognize it in advance and determine that you can ride out the dry spells.

Any fund that lacks consistency will give you some major gut checks over the years. What's worse, it will give you reason to doubt and second-guess your buying decisions, which leads to more decisionmaking problems down the road.

MANAGERIAL STABILITY

The average diversified equity fund keeps the same manager for just over three years, but numerous studies have shown that funds that consistently beat the Standard & Poor's 500 Index have an average manager tenure of ten years.

As the fund industry has evolved, it has become increasingly difficult to find those long-term managers. Fund managers might break off to start their own funds, be lured away to different firms or to hedge funds, or might simply retire. As a result, investors who want an actively managed fund can find stability in a few ways.

You can start by looking for a manager with a long and consistent track record, even if it is with more than one fund. Garrett Van Wagoner, for example, runs his eponymous fund family in the exact same fashion as he ran Govett Smaller Companies Fund, which is where he first made his reputation as a stock picker.

Another choice is to look for a fund family that has the proverbial "deep bench," meaning they have a history of replacing star managers without missing a beat. This would apply to most of the big fund companies, where managers are succeeded by colleagues or analysts with whom they worked for years. This kind of orderly succession means a smooth transition for a fund and no investment surprises for shareholders. The time to get nervous as a shareholder is when you see a manager change and the new blood has a discipline completely different from the old.

This is also why you want to see stability in the manager's research and support team. Sometimes, star managers will break out and start their own fund but leave behind helpers and assistants; in some cases, the public then finds out just how important that staff was to a manager's success.

If a fund company shakes up its research team or brings in a new chief investment officer whose style is not in keeping with how the fund has been run in the past, management stability could be a problem.

Yet another option for providing management is the team approach, where a fund is run by several advisers. The advantage here is that the team goes on and moves forward even as one player moves up or out. The downside, according to some critics of team-management approach, is that management by consensus can make it harder for a fund to make bold moves.

ACCOUNTABILITY

Good funds stand up for their actions and take responsibility for their decisions. They don't blame the market for their problems, because there are good opportunities in every market, even when their chosen specialty is out of favor.

As discussed, team management can breed stability, but it hurts some funds in the accountability area. Individual managers follow their own convictions, whereas a team might squabble over a fund's direction. Although many experts believe managers benefit from knowing that investors hold them personally responsible, this belief can't be quantified.

That kind of motivation can't hurt.

Regardless of the management style, you want a fund that offers someone to tell you what's going on in terms that you understand and that help convince you the fund is worth owning in good times and bad.

When managers start making excuses rather than reminding you that they believe in their investment strategy and want to stick to their discipline, the fund is in trouble.

WRONG-WAY SIGNS

If all of the funds you are interested in show up only at the top of the one-year performance charts but never seem to carry that record on for five or ten years, it's a clear sign that you have placed too high a priority on what a fund has done lately and not enough on whether it's worth owning for a lifetime.

> *How quickly investors flock to better-performing mutual funds, even though financial researchers have shown that the hot funds in one time period very often turn out to be the poorest performers in another.*
>
> —FUND MANAGER DAVID DREMAN,
> *The New Contrarian Investment Strategy*

6 section

CHARACTERISTICS OF A LOSING FUND

THE PREVIOUS CHAPTER COVERED SOME COMMON TRAITS of successful mutual funds. As an investor, it would be tempting to take that list and assume that it will automatically lead you to great funds. But it doesn't always work that way. You see, there is an equally distinct set of characteristics for fund losers and, to complicate matters, some funds carry both sets of traits. You could find, for example, a fund with a consistent style but high expenses that slow performance. The average fund, in fact, has some balance of these winning and losing characteristics, which explains why the fund is, well, average.

> You're looking for funds that have the qualities that lead to superior performance without the bad habits that lead to mediocrity.

The object, therefore, is not only to check off successful traits but also to eliminate any fund that carries the troublesome ones.

It's not that a fund can't overcome one or more of the problem areas—in fact, many funds beat high costs long enough to top the charts—but they can't necessarily defeat those demons year after year. That's why the following bad traits are almost always visible at the bottom of *long-term* performance charts but absent in funds at the top.

HIGH EXPENSES

As previously noted, there are thousands of mutual funds, but not so many ways to actually manage a fund. In fact, funds in the same asset class are often very similar, with the majority of their performance being attributed to owning the same stocks. What separates similar funds is their expense ratio. For example, two funds may be relatively similar in style and performance, with both buying large-company growth stocks, but one fund may have an expense ratio of 1.0 percent, while the other has a ratio of 2.0 percent. Chances are you'll gravitate toward the fund with the lower cost to you.

> Expense ratios are the total costs shareholders pay annually to cover the fund's operating costs and management fees. See Section 13 for more details.

If large-cap growth stocks return 10 percent, the funds will earn that gain minus expenses. On the higher-cost fund, therefore, you actually lose 20 percent of the profits you made from putting your money into that particular segment of the market. And while a 1.0-percent difference in expenses might seem insignificant, it isn't. The manager trying to overcome the higher expense ratio may take bigger risks, trying to implement strategies that make up for the cost handicap. Eventually, that kind of gamble tends to backfire. A 2.0-percent expense ratio is not so bad when a fund has been earning 20 percent, but if you have a 5-percent loss—which the additional costs turn into a 7-percent loss—you can easily understand why investors dislike high costs.

As a general rule, bond fund expenses should fall in the range of 0.5 percent to 1.0 percent. Stock funds are most desirable when the expense ratio is no more than 1.5 percent, but preferable at 1 percent or below. This includes all ongoing costs, including sales and marketing (12b-1) fees. About the only high-expense funds that may be worth considering are exotic or esoteric funds, such as those that invest in so-called emerging markets, where the costs of doing research to find the best investments in some far-flung part of the world justify the bigger fee paid to management.

EXCESSIVE TURNOVER

It's important to note there are some very good funds that have high turnover, so this characteristic is not always inherently negative. But funds that move rapid-fire from one stock to the next sometimes hurt their performance; frequently, even if their returns hold up, the investor actually suffers.

Obviously, the more a fund trades, the less it allows buy-and-hold strategies to work, and the simple own-it-and-keep-it strategy has proven to be the most successful means to bigger returns for most people, individuals and pros alike. But what trading also does is erode the tax efficiency of a fund. Those trades are taxable events, and the fund's capital gains are part of your annual tax obligation.

Yes, a fund could offset its gains by selling losers and, no, not every high-turnover fund is tax inefficient. Beyond that, though, tax efficiency becomes irrelevant if you hold the fund in a retirement account. Still, if your fund gains 10 percent in a year but half of that money is in the form of capital gains, the fund's real, after-tax return is not so good. Of your annual gain, in this example, 5 percent gets distributed to you, and as much as 40 percent of that will go to Uncle Sam and his Federal and State Tax Band. You pay that tax—even if you simply reinvest the gains and dividends—and your real after-tax return is somewhere in the neighborhood of 8 percent.

Over time, that can be a costly haircut.

When looking at funds for taxable accounts, therefore, examine turnover. If the number is high, check out the fund's history of paying out capital-gains distributions to see whether Uncle Sam would get a big chunk of your profits if you bought the fund.

MARKET TIMING

Funds that engage in market timing can be like the old cliché about patrons in a late-night singles bar; they look good at first glance but aren't nearly so attractive in the harsh light of day.

These funds often top the performance charts during the good times, and it is only by examining the fund's stated investment strategy or reading the manager's statements that you uncover the market-timing elements, often disguised as saying the fund will "move toward safety" in an uncertain market.

The trouble with a market-timing fund is that it typically sells out of stocks and moves into cash early, before a downturn occurs. If and when the downturn actually arrives, the fund is sitting pretty because it has cash and bonds earning a small but respectable return whereas the funds still holding stocks are headed south for a while. It's on the upswing that market-timers tend to look bad, staying in cash too long or wrongly predicting a downturn when none happens, at which point they stay on the sidelines while the market goes higher.

Occasionally, managers will hold more cash because they can't find anything the fits their investment criteria. But beware of any managers who openly plan to routinely seek high ground whenever they foresee bad times; the aggregate performance history of funds that time the market says these issues will be inconsistent and volatile and deliver below-average returns in the long term.

> Typically, the funds that do the best are those that are fully invested and put their money to work in the style and asset class they specialize in.

PUNITIVE OR RESTRICTIVE FEES AND POLICIES

This is a mixed message, because *some* restrictive policies are actually good for shareholders. Short-term redemption fees, for example, correctly punish investors who jump in and out of a fund. This is positive for long-term shareholders because it discourages the kind of quick turnarounds that can force a manager to make ill-timed moves.

But be aware that many funds, particularly small ones, require a signature guarantee rather than a phone call to opt out or come with a fee for closing the account, regardless of time frame. When a fund charges excessive termination fees or layers in ways to nickel-and-dime its customers, it is proving that it is less interested in you as an owner and more interested in shaking you down at every available opportunity. Read the prospectus carefully to make sure you understand how to get in and out of the fund and look at any one-time fees that might apply to moving money around. In all of the years I have covered mutual funds, all of the oddball restrictive keep-the-money-in-the-fund policies I have come across have belonged to the worst funds. Good funds don't need to play these games.

SENSELESS INVESTMENT POLICIES

This can mean many different things. It could be something like the Stock Car Stock Index Fund, which invests only in companies that support auto racing (but which considers a company like McDonald's to be an auto-racing stock because it sponsors race cars), or it could be virtually any small-cap value or small-cap contrarian fund, most of which proved in the late 1990s that there may not be enough stocks in their little realm to actually build a viable fund.

But although this is hard to define, it is a bit like pornography, in that you will know it when you see it. If a fund has an investment strategy that you can't explain to your spouse in two sentences, something is amiss. If it takes you another two sentences to justify the fund's strategy, something is just plain wrong.

The best funds are straightforward investments. They buy stocks or bonds, or both, from specific portions of the investment world. They look for certain characteristics in those investments, in order to deliver reasonable, above average, consistent (and so on) returns to shareholders. Anything beyond that and you need to start looking at what the fund is really doing. Returns often vary inversely to the amount of time the fund manager spends explaining his investment policy.

THE RIGHT WAY TO PROCEED

Trust your gut. If something strikes you as not being quite right, eliminate the fund from your selection process. With thousands of mutual funds out there, you can always find a fund that buys the assets you want without saddling you with a bad feeling about how the manager or the fund company is going to act.

You may not feel like you know a lot about funds, but if you know enough to be even the slightest bit nervous that a fund's bad traits may come shining through, then you know enough to steer clear.

INVESTMENT OBJECTIVES

MOST PEOPLE ASSUME THAT THEIR INVESTMENT OBJECTIVE pretty much matches that of their mutual funds. The logic is simple: The fund wants to make money. They want you to make money. That's a match. If investing were that simple, however, you wouldn't need this book. Truth be told, funds have one set of investment objectives, whereas individuals have another. The trick is laying the objectives of the fund over your personal goals to find out where you and the fund have enough in common.

First, let's look at the standard investment objectives for individuals. Realistically, there are three different goals that most investors have for their money:

1. Growth of capital
2. Preservation of capital
3. Maximizing income

If you are looking for growth, you should choose stock mutual funds. If preservation of capital is your concern, you will turn to funds that mix stocks and bonds (or you will do the mixing yourself), and if your aim is to maximize income, you will use either bonds or bond funds.

Just as objectives vary, there are also a variety of ways to *achieve* these financial goals. You can shoot for slow-and-steady returns that try to provide consistency in all market conditions, or you can race out and try for the best possible returns in the shortest possible time frame, therefore injecting more volatility into your investment portfolio.

Your funds, meanwhile, have investment objectives that are tied not only to your goals but also to the type of assets they buy. On the surface, funds come in a variety of flavors that by their very name, imply that they serve to meet a specific objective: growth, growth and income, value, capital appreciation, aggressive growth, international, all sorts of bond funds, and many other types.

But no matter what the type of fund is, the investment objective laid out in its prospectus will provide a basic and candid description of how the fund actually achieves its goals and where it falls within those three individual investment objectives.

> Sections 8 and 9 detail specifics on fund types and investment styles.

The prospectus wording will read something like this: "The fund will seek growth of capital by investing substantially all of its assets—but no less than 80 percent—in the common stocks of large companies." The fund's investment objective will most likely go on to say the fund can invest, for example, in foreign securities, derivatives, private stock, and other investment vehicles. That important information may also be buried deeper in the prospectus under "investment policy."

In short, the fund's paperwork tells you little other than that it is interested in "growth of capital" and investment in "stocks of large companies." Yes, some fund companies go farther with their statements, but you just don't get a whole lot to go on. It's never enough information to conclude: "This fund is trying to be so aggressive that I'd be better off playing lottery scratch tickets with the kids' college money." Still, if you can pick up some of the key traits or characteristics that the fund uses to describe itself, you have a start.

Next, examine the telltale signs of how the fund actually accomplishes its mission. Without getting too deeply into investment styles, the question becomes whether the fund is racing to meet its objectives, looking always to top the performance charts, or shooting for something that's a bit safer and more toward the middle of the pack. The fund's track record will graphically show you the consistency with which the fund has achieved its objective in any given year. And as previously mentioned, the investment objective or investment policy will state specifically what the fund is allowed to purchase. Therefore, you are looking not only for a fund with a stated objective that matches your own but for one that shows performance consistent with what you can stomach and that buys assets that enhance the rest of your portfolio.

To build a diversified mutual-fund portfolio, you will want to combine funds that meet your objective and risk tolerance while covering different parts of the investment world. Thus, you might want one fund that invests in large-company stocks, another that pursues small companies, and maybe a third that invests in international stocks. Having too many funds that do the same thing is likely to dampen the overall return of your portfolio.

Unless you plan to buy a one-size-fits-all fund, where the manager tries to do everything for an investor, you will have to look for an investment objective as it relates to the assets being purchased. Some large-cap funds, for example, invest in stocks that have above-average dividends and try to make dividend income a significant contributor to the fund's total return. Companies with big dividends tend to be slow growers, whereas many fast-growth companies pay no attention to dividend income.

> Remember, turn the fund's best year upside down and consider that as a possible loss—that would be the fund's worst-case scenario.

So, if your aim is growth, you will want to look for a mix of funds that seek "growth of capital" by investing in stocks of various sizes. You can gauge your expectations according to what various types of investments have delivered in the past. According to Ibbotson Associates, the Chicago-based investment research firm, the average annual return on both large- and small-company stocks has been roughly 13 percent since 1970. It has been closer to 12 percent for international stocks, 9.8 percent for both long-term corporate and government bonds, and 6.5 percent for Treasury bills.

As long as one keeps in mind that past performance is no great predictor of the future—T-bills spent the late 1990s closer to 4 percent than to 7 percent, for example—it is possible to develop an investment plan by choosing funds that share your investment objectives and follow the investment style you determine works best for you.

THE LEAST YOU SHOULD REMEMBER

Pick a fund first and foremost because it meets your investment objective. Before setting out to buy a fund, sit down and take a look at the role you want this investable money to play, the job it is supposed to do within your portfolio. This will point you to the right kinds of funds.

THE RIGHT WAY TO PROCEED

Start by examining a fund's investment objective, then move to how it plans to accomplish that objective. You will learn a lot about a fund and whether it truly interests you by looking at these elements before you consider performance.

> *If you don't know where you're going, you'll end up somewhere else.*
>
> —Yogi Berra,
> Hall of Fame baseball player and manager

TYPES OF FUNDS

THERE WAS A TIME WHEN YOU COULD LEARN virtually everything there was to know about a fund just by its name. Sadly for investors, that time ended about two decades ago. After that, when savvy investors noticed something significant about a fund's name, it was usually because of celebrated blowups that highlighted a major inconsistency between what the name evoked and what the fund actually invested in.

Consider Alliance North American Government Income Fund, for example, which suffered severe losses during the Mexican currency crisis of the mid-1990s. The problem occurred because of the fund's investments in Argentina—not only because those investments went haywire but because Argentina is not in North America. Investors learned from this experience that unless otherwise constrained by its prospectus, a mutual fund needs to keep only 65 percent of its holdings in the assets for which it is named. That means that a real-estate fund could, for example, go out and buy technology stocks in an effort to goose flagging returns. Likewise, a small-company stock fund could buy large stocks with at least a portion of its portfolio.

There is frequent inconsistency between how a fund is named and how it invests. For example, the dearth of dividends paid out by most of the high-flying stocks of the 1990s has meant that most growth-and-income funds disdain the income side of their equation in favor of concentrating on growth. Their returns throughout the 1990s improved as a result, but they did not deliver what investors might have been seeking if they wanted a measure of income and heightened safety compared to funds that were all-out growth oriented.

The preceding chapter noted the importance of checking out a fund's investment objective and investment policy. I'll reinforce that here, because the basics of picking a type of fund do not always tell you how the fund pursues that goal. Not all "growth funds" are created equal.

TYPES OF FUNDS

Funds are categorized in a number of different ways, specifically by broad investment types and by the size of the stocks or bonds they invest in. In broad terms—which is how funds are named and categorized—here are the most common types of funds and what you can expect from each.

> Once you have decided on the type of fund you want and are comparing two or more choices, the funds' investment policies may become a deciding factor in which fund you feel most comfortable with.

Growth Funds

This gets confusing because the term "growth" has two meanings here. It can signal that the fund invests in the "growth" investment style, buying stocks of companies that show some type of consistent growth (sales, earnings, and so on), or it can mean that the aim of this fund is simply "growth," as in helping your money to grow. Regardless of definition, a growth fund should be one that invests entirely in stocks and that plans to grow as those issues appreciate, rather than through dividends.

Growth-and-Income Funds

Add an income component from dividends to your basic growth fund and the result is a growth-and-income fund. As previously mentioned, however, the paucity of dividends paid out during the bull market of the 1990s has made "growth-and-income" something of a misnomer, as most of these issues are really "growth-but-no-income" funds.

With that in mind, it's fair to say that most growth-and-income funds are no longer true to their objective. Instead, "growth-and-income" has become a euphemism for "more conservative than the growth fund." In general, the same basic style applies—and many fund families have tremendous overlap between their growth and growth-and-income funds—but with an eye on providing steadier, less-volatile returns than the growth fund.

Aggressive Growth or Capital Appreciation Funds

Again, using the basic growth fund as a standard, these funds are designed to shoot for even higher returns, usually by investing in small-company and less-mature stocks. On the scale of a fund company's offerings, its capital appreciation or aggressive growth fund is typically the most risky diversified fund in the lot. The one exception to that would be if the fund family offers sector funds.

Sector Funds

These are funds that are designed to invest entirely in one business or industry, such as technology or Internet companies, health-care firms, utilities, and the like. Although diversified within an industry by holding a wide range of companies, these funds tend to be more volatile than the average growth fund because they are concentrated in a single business area.

At times when the economy favors, say, health-care stocks, a health-care fund is likely to boom. Just as quickly, however, the economy can turn and the entire sector can be dragged down. Sector funds frequently top the one- and three-year performance lists, which is why they are so attractive. What most investors overlook is that sector funds—from those areas that are out of favor—most often run at the bottom of those charts, too.

Balanced Funds

These funds try to serve up a mix of stocks and bonds. As a result, the rules concerning what percent of the holdings must be in stocks or bonds are a bit different. By rule, a balanced fund is supposed to have at least 25 percent of its portfolio in stocks and 25 percent in bonds. The remaining half of the money can be invested either way, and managers typically will go where the getting is good, loading up on stocks when the market is booming and on bonds during the downturns.

On the risk-reward scale, these funds fall somewhere below growth-and-income funds. The bonds make these funds less volatile and risky but also limit the potential gains of the fund.

International Funds

This is the extremely broad category of funds that invest their money overseas. The key here is to see where the money is invested, because it could be in big international blue-chip companies, or it might be in tiny foreign aggressive-growth companies. Key subgroups among international funds are *single-country funds* (similar to sector funds, except that they invest in one country rather than one industry) and *emerging-markets funds*, which pursue their profits in smaller, developing nations.

Global Funds

These are international funds with one significant twist: They can keep a significant portion of their money invested in domestic stocks. As a result, if they find that the most attractive stock market offerings are on Wall Street, the portfolio may reflect mostly the performance of U.S. stocks rather than international companies.

That flexibility is good, if you want a fund manager to decide how much of your money is invested abroad. If, however, you want to set your asset allocation and diversify a percentage of your money internationally, a global fund may not actually achieve your goals.

Convertible Securities Funds

You can find convertible securities funds in the same flavors—sector, large company, and so forth—as other funds, but what makes them unique is that the manager buys convertible securities instead of stocks. Convertibles are a hybrid investment that most often comes in the form of interest-paying bonds (although it can be preferred stock) that can be swapped for shares of the issuing company's stock at a predetermined price.

The bondlike yield facet of a convertible protects against stock declines, while the ability to convert into stock offers shelter against falling bond prices.

The idea is to capture about two-thirds of stock market returns with half of the downside risk so that, in theory, a diversified convertible fund would gain 6.6 percent for every 10-percent market rise, but fall just 5 percent during a 10-percent market correction.

Convertible funds have never been particularly popular, due largely to the fact that savvy investors don't buy what they don't understand—and most people haven't got a clue about the workings of convertibles. But in the 1990s, convertible bond funds also suffered by not being able to deliver what they promised, namely downside protection and lower risk; in fact, the convertible market is small and has limited high-quality choices, which has caused some managers to juice their portfolios with junk bonds and derivative securities that can actually increase risk and volatility. If you are considering a convertible fund, be particularly careful in reading the prospectus and look to see if the manager shows any bias toward acting more like a stock or bond fund so that you can shape your expectations accordingly.

Money-Market Funds

The safest of all mutual funds, these resemble a checking account more than your average stock mutual fund. Money-market mutual funds invest in safe, liquid securities like bank certificates of deposit, government securities, high-grade corporate financing agreements and other commercial paper that pays money-market interest rates, and the rules governing money funds are so tight that virtually all of them deliver roughly the same performance.

Some money funds create tax and safety benefits by purchasing only certain assets, such as municipal, government, or insured bonds. Others carry insurance to protect the fund company in the event of a credit crisis.

> Unlike most other types of fund accounts, money funds generally have check-writing privileges and other features that make them a safe haven for your emergency and short-term investment monies.

High-Yield Bond Funds

This is a mutual-fund euphemism, because though fund marketers may say "high-yield bonds," what they really mean is "junk bonds." The bonds do indeed deliver a higher return than government securities, but at much higher risk. Junk bonds get their name because they buy corporate securities that the major bond-rating agencies see as having significant default risk.

That doesn't mean these funds always lose money, because they don't. In fact, junk-bond funds often do exactly what they are supposed to, bringing back an extra point or two of return compared to other long-term bond funds. Still, investors who would normally shy away from high-risk investments should not be suckered in by a fund promising high yields—investors need to look out for how those yields are really achieved.

> Junk bonds are considered "below investment quality."

Government-Bond Funds

There are many subsets here, ranging from funds that buy only Treasury bonds to those that invest only in municipal bonds to those that buy only bonds issued in a single state (which can make the fund double- or triple-tax-free) to international bond funds. The key to understanding a bond fund is finding out what it invests in and what the tax ramifications are for you. For example, several fund companies offer Florida single-state bond funds, which, surprisingly, have sold quite well. The reason this is surprising is that Florida has no state income tax, so that there is no reason to buy a bond fund that avoids paying state income tax there. Logically, a Florida investor might prefer to pick high-quality, better yielding bond issues from a wider pool of investments, expressly because they have no state income tax to worry about.

> For more on expenses, see Section 13.

The other issue with bond funds is expenses. While costs are important in every type of fund, they are crucial with bonds, where countless studies have shown that the difference between the performance of funds in the same asset class tends to be equal to the difference between the expense ratios of the funds.

In many Treasury funds, which are designed to invest in nothing outside of U.S. Treasury bonds, notes, and bills, the fund manager simply buys the proscribed type of security and doesn't even manage the maturity of the overall portfolio. In those cases, funds tend to be very similar, and their purchase tends to be more about safety and security than growth of assets.

Other types of bond funds range from the volatile zero-coupon or target-maturity funds—essentially betting on the direction of interest rates, which makes for extremely volatile funds, as well as those that buy corporate bonds, convertible securities, and junk.

Index Funds

Many investors consider these funds to be their very own group, but technically, that is not the case. Index funds come in virtually all of the aforementioned fund types. You can buy index funds for large-growth stocks, international stocks, or any other type of investing for which there is an index to measure performance.

If you are attracted to index investing, you need to look for index funds that cover the various market segments in order to be fully diversified. But owning several index funds does not make you any more diversified than owning several growth mutual funds; it is the underlying assets—the designated index— that determine the quality of the fund.

> Indexing describes a style of investing rather than an asset class.

One key alternative to the index fund is known as the "exchange-traded fund" or "index share." Essentially, this is a security that acts like a fund but trades like a stock. The most commonly known variety is the "Spider," or Standard & Poor's Depositary Receipt (SPDR).

Because they trade like stocks and offer intraday pricing and the ability to place limit orders—where you pay a specific price or bail out when a certain price target is reached—index shares are worth considering as an alternative to funds. Just as fund companies are always developing new flavors of fund, so new types of index shares are evolving, but they have now reached the point where they are a viable alternative for anyone who has decided to make the index choice.

> A Spider mimics the S&P 500 Index.

Flexible-Portfolio Funds

These are the "go-anywhere funds" that follow the manager's instincts across the established lines of the other types of funds. In some cases, they may change asset classes entirely based on the market-timing decisions of the manager. In other cases, the manager simply goes where he or she finds bargains, which could be undervalued small companies one week and Brazilian currency trading the next.

Any fund that is described this way should force you to look at the portfolio, both as it exists now and as it looked in the past (through either old fund paperwork or a research firm's history of the fund's holdings). It might look like a mid-cap growth fund today, but it could have been small-cap value twelve months ago.

Asset-Allocation and Life-Cycle Funds

These are designed to be one-size-fits-all funds, created specifically for investors of a certain age group. The idea is that the fund will get more conservative as you near retirement. Before picking one of these funds—and they are popular choices in many retirement plans—be sure you understand how the fund will change over time and make sure you agree with the strategy.

Social-Investment Funds

Funds calling themselves "socially responsible"—a name I disdain because it implies that all other funds are irresponsible—attract investors who don't want to own companies that pollute, sell products that are hazardous to society's health, and so on. Social funds buy only stocks and bonds that meet the management's political or social agenda.

> The potential problem with life-cycle funds is that the fund's asset allocation many not be your own; it could be too conservative or aggressive for your tastes.

That said, social funds actually fall into the other categories rather than being a stand-alone group. You can buy social-growth funds, balanced funds, aggressive-growth funds, and so forth. If you want to be a social investor, therefore, construct your asset allocation as usual. When you go to pick funds within a category, however, look only at the social choices. Realize, too, that screening out society's bad actors raises costs, which eats away at returns, and that returns may be dampened by a social fund's decision to avoid high-growth sectors like gaming or tobacco.

ASSET SIZE AND INVESTMENT STYLE

Now that we've examined the basic fund types, we'll look at another way of slicing and dicing funds, specifically *asset size* and *investment style*.

"Market capitalization" refers to the total number of outstanding shares in a stock multiplied by its current stock price. The result is a measure of a company's size based on its total market value. From a fund-investment standpoint, however, "cap sizes" tell you the types of stocks a fund buys and whether it tends toward large or small companies. This then allows you to set your return expectations, in accordance with historical performance data—the famous Ibbotson-Sinquefield study that shows that stocks, over time, return roughly 10 percent per year also shows that small caps tend to do a little better than that, but with more volatility.

Understanding the implications of market cap also allows you to diversify your portfolio to cover all segments of the market. In the old days, you might have bought three growth funds, only to find that they all bought the same types of assets; today, you can buy a small-cap, mid-cap, and large-cap growth fund to better diversify your portfolio.

Providing a definition of cap sizes is a bit tricky, especially given the market's growth during the 1990s. Halfway through the decade, many observers still considered a $1-billion company to be a "large cap," when stock market growth had already made the $1-billion club of stocks enormous. But if you look at research firms like Frank Russell Company, Morningstar, Inc., and Lipper, Inc., their definitions of different cap sizes boil down into something that can change over time, which looks like this:

"Giant caps," some of which fold into the large-cap category, are the biggest of the big, roughly the 100 largest companies on the market. At this writing, "giant cap" would apply to any company with a total market value in excess of $40 billion.

"Large cap" has a variety of definitions. Some believe the sector encompasses "blue-chip" stocks, which would make it at least as big as the Standard & Poor's 500 Index, whereas others believe that it should be loosely defined as including the 1,000 largest stocks or that it applies to one-third of all companies. At this writing, "large cap" could be used loosely to describe those stocks with a total market value of $10 billion and up.

"Mid cap" applies to the next grouping of stocks. Frank Russell Co., for example, defines large caps as the first 200 stocks in the Russell 1000—its index of the largest stocks by market capitalization—with mid-cap stocks making up the next 800. In spite of the fact that mid caps outnumber large caps, they don't represent as much of the market's total value. The large-cap stocks represent about three-fourths of the total value of the Russell 1000, with mid caps making up the rest. A stock is generally considered to be a mid cap once its market value exceeds $1.5 billion up to large-cap size.

Market Caps

Giant caps	$40 billion+
Large caps	$10 billion+
Mid caps	$1.5 billion+
Small caps	$250 million+
Micro caps	below $250 million

"Small cap" can loosely be applied to everything that's left over, although the micro-cap category is usually applied to stocks with less than $250 million in market value.

Lastly, "multi cap" is a new term coined by Lipper, Inc. in 1999 to apply to funds that don't strictly adhere to any cap size. These types of funds look for specific things in their investments—growth stocks, for example, regardless of cap size. The result is a fund that really can't be pigeonholed into any of the other categories, akin to a "flexible-portfolio fund" in that it follows the manager's whim more than any mandate to buy a specific size of assets.

Ultimately, when you combine a fund's overall strategy with the size of assets it buys, you wind up with useful information when it comes to allocating assets. Morningstar, for example, divvies up funds into "style-boxes," which look like tic-tac-toe grids and categorize a fund by both its investment style and asset size, as in "large-cap growth fund." Lipper, Inc. uses an even bigger grid, to account for those multi-cap funds.

In buying a fund, no matter where prospectus materials say it falls, examine these style measures to make sure you are getting what you pay for.

THE RIGHT WAY TO PROCEED

Construct a portfolio that helps you cover a wide spectrum of investment objectives or that fills in the various boxes in the Morningstar or Lipper style grids.

WRONG-WAY SIGNS

When your fund does something that its peer funds did not do, something is up. If you own a real-estate fund that shows big profits at a time when real-estate funds are generally down, you should take the time to examine its investment assets. Likewise, if your fund is down when the rest of the category is up, there's a problem that requires further scrutiny.

The fastest way for a fund to get noticed in its category is to do something that is out of character for its peers, essentially to "game" the system, meaning that the fund promises to do one thing but actually takes a different strategy. Good or bad, if your fund presents a surprise compared to its peers, you need to examine the fund more closely. The fund you own may not be investing the way you wanted it to when you bought it.

9

INVESTMENT STYLES

ONCE YOU KNOW WHAT A FUND BUYS, you need to know the way it actually goes about picking those investments.

That's all a question of style. Some fund managers chase momentum, buying only those stocks where sales or earnings are on the rise. Others look for bargains, hoping to find stocks that are underpriced but that the market will soon discover and bid up.

When it comes to investment styles, there are several key questions:

- Growth, value, or blend?
- Top-down or bottom-up?
- Active or passive?
- Focused or diversified?

You must actually answer each of the above questions when selecting a fund. What's more, as you develop a fund portfolio, you will want it to reflect different investment styles as well as diverse investments.

GROWTH, VALUE, OR BLEND?

The last section pointed out that funds aren't always what they are named for, and this is a case in point. There are "growth funds" that actually follow the value style of investing, and then there are "growth funds" in which the name is both descriptive of the fund's general mission and its investment style.

Yes, that's confusing.

Funds that follow the growth style of investing seek out companies that combine high rates of growth with rising profits. Typically, these companies are growing at a rate faster than the economy. Growth stocks tend to have high price-to-earnings ratios—a comparison of stock price to profits—because above-average potential warrants higher prices. Furthermore, growth managers don't worry much about price because they believe the growth will fuel price appreciation. Besides, if you ask a growth investor, something that is cheap could be underpriced for a good reason—and it could stay that way.

> Michael Price, the value investor and former manager of the Mutual Series funds, was famous for buying into troubled companies and helping to jump-start a turnaround.

Funds that follow the value style of investing, by comparison, look for stocks that are cheap relative to the value of their assets. A value fund manager will make this appraisal by examining the stock's balance sheet and estimating how much the company would be worth if it were broken into pieces. Typically, value stocks have a high dividend yield and a low price-to-earnings ratio; they may come from market sectors that are "out of favor" and may even be troubled companies that have gone into bankruptcy. How deep into the well a value manager will dive depends on the individual tendencies of the manager.

In general, growth investing offers the highest potential reward, but with more volatility. Value investors surrender some profit potential for a smoother ride. But that is not true all of the time. In the late 1990s, value investing was in a deep hole, troubled enough for many investors to question whether this investment philosophy was worth pursuing at all. Over time, however, both growth and value tend to have their favorable cycles.

> Many financial advisers suggest investing in both value and growth to diversify a portfolio.

Ironically, when a value stock heats up and rewards the investor, it also tends to change characteristics. Typically, it shows sales and earnings growth and, over time, morphs into a growth stock. At that point, a true value investor sells the stock and captures profits (with the likely buyer being a growth manager).

This is where a "blend" style enters the picture. As you might imagine from the name, a blend fund will own both growth and value stocks, tilting toward value when it can fund underpriced stocks but letting its winners run as they become growth stocks over time.

Another blend style is known as GARP, an acronym for "growth at a reasonable price." Essentially, a manager practicing GARP buys growth stocks that aren't too expensive, letting value investing tinge the selection process. In short, GARP investors put limits on what they will pay for growth. This, for example, might mean buying companies with earnings growth rates equal to the Standard & Poor's 500 but price-to-earnings ratios less than the index, where the traditional growth manager would not be concerned with sticking to low P/E stocks. Critics say that GARP is just an easy excuse for a growth manager to buy value stocks or for a value manager to buy growth stocks.

TOP-DOWN OR BOTTOM-UP?

These are two distinct approaches for actually selecting stocks.

Top-down investing starts with an investor looking at general economic trends and deciding which sectors and industries will benefit from those developments. Having identified potential hot spots, the investor picks stocks that capitalize on the trends. An investor forecasting high inflation, for example, might expect mining to pick up and would scour the mining industry for the stocks that stand to benefit most from rising prices.

The opposite approach, bottom-up investing, involves selecting outstanding companies first, before considering economic trends. This method assumes that an individual company can thrive even when its industry does not. A growth-fund manager who applies a bottom-up approach, therefore, will look for fast-growth companies regardless of the industry they are in.

> Typically, top-down funds tend to do some market timing, moving significant assets into a sector that the manager's research shows as being ready to pop.

ACTIVE OR PASSIVE?

Beyond the style of stock picking, investors have to choose whether they want to have a manager actively picking stocks or whether they prefer instead to use an index fund to deliver the return of the asset class they are investing in.

An index fund is set up to mirror a specific stock market benchmark, from the Standard & Poor's 500 to the small-cap Russell 2000, from the Domini Social Equity Index (which combines an index structure with social investing) to the Stock Car Stock Index (which supposedly gives you the companies behind auto racing).

Index funds can also come with a growth- or value-investing tilt, meaning that the management company starts by replicating an index like the S&P 500 but then only holds the growth or value stocks from within that index. Replicating the index provides certain key benefits, starting with low costs. A fund that is passively managed doesn't need to have the research and trading costs of its actively managed peers.

> In an index fund, costs represent "friction," the only thing that slows a fund from keeping pace with a benchmark.

Therefore, if an index jumps 20 percent, an investor in a fund tied to that index would expect to have a return of roughly 19.5 to 19.8 percent, depending on the expense ratio of the particular fund. The lower the cost, the less friction, and the closer the fund comes to meeting its benchmark. In short, index funds typically have expense ratios anywhere from one-tenth to one-half the size of the average actively managed fund.

> An expense ratio represents the percentage of your investment that is paid annually to cover the fund's management fees and operating costs.

Index funds are also tax efficient. Because they seldom trade securities within the portfolio, index funds seldom have capital gains to distribute. That makes them an ideal choice for buy-and-hold investors, who can let their money grow without having significant tax liabilities along the way.

The downside of index fund investing is that you are guaranteed to have a decline in your portfolio any time the market goes down—no one minds being tied to a balloon, but it's not so nice feeling tied to an anchor—and you can't "beat the market," which is the preoccupation of many investors. America is not a country of people who enjoy finishing second, and many investors prefer to take a shot at getting returns better than what the market can deliver.

That's where active management adds value. Although not every actively managed fund is designed to beat the market—some are built to offer protection and stability in down markets—the idea behind active management is that research and investment acumen can lead a fund to own the best of what is available within its chosen asset class.

Although active management certainly is more interesting and entertaining, the problem is that such research costs money, leading to higher expense ratios.

Active management can also result in more rapid trading of stocks, which can generate capital gains that get passed along to investors and result in tax bills. Consequently, active management often lags behind the very indexes it is supposed to beat. Throughout much of the 1990s, for example, roughly one in ten active fund managers were able to beat the Standard & Poor's 500 (though, in fairness, the S&P is not a fair benchmark for all of those funds).

> Nobel Prize–winning economist Paul Samuelson once estimated that an active manager must beat the market by two percentage points just to come out even after expenses.

There are plenty of experts—most notably Peter Lynch, the legendary former manager of Fidelity Magellan—who note that this tends to run in cycles and that active management will have stretches where it seems more likely to work; but it is hard to argue against the long-term success of a buy-and-hold strategy involving index funds.

One way to attempt to beat the market—as well as to develop a well-rounded portfolio—is to make index funds a core holding and then build around them. This "core-and-explore" philosophy guarantees that a big chunk of your money will deliver market returns, which one hopes could be enhanced by a few select choices from a mix of asset categories.

FOCUSED OR DIVERSIFIED?

Diversification is supposed to be one of the big benefits of fund investing, but that does not mean that every fund needs to be diversified. Focused or concentrated funds own just a few stocks—ostensibly the manager's best bets—and hope to turbocharge performance by holding larger positions of a small number of issues.

By law, diversified funds—more than 90 percent of all funds available today—own a lot of stocks. Three-fourths of a fund's portfolio must be divvied up so that no single issue amounts to more than 5 percent of the fund. Generally, it's carte blanche with the rest, but most managers keep all positions far below the 5-percent line.

In funds that don't own many stocks—and it takes a minimum of sixteen stocks to meet those diversification rules—managers must also sometimes pull their flowers and water the weeds, pruning winners to stay diversified, while holding less-successful stocks in order to remain fully invested.

Nondiversified funds, by comparison, can generally hold up to half of their portfolio in a single issue and do not face the 5-percent limit on smaller holdings. That means the manager can focus on a few issues and let winners grow unabated. A nondiversified manager employing a buy-and-hold strategy may need no more than a handful of good ideas in an entire year.

That doesn't require that every nondiversified fund hold just a few stocks. Diversification, in this case, is something of a legal matter, disclosed in the prospectus. A fund may say it is not a diversified fund—which gives it the right to hold fewer than sixteen stocks—but may still hold thirty to fifty issues if that suits the manager's needs. Likewise, you may find a fund described in the prospectus as diversified, but the manager might state a plan to own no more than about two dozen stocks, a strategy that is hardly the same as owning a few hundred.

Still, any fund that holds fewer than a few dozen stocks is living by the axiom "It's a market of stocks, not a stock market." But concentrating a portfolio can also make a fund overheat and blow up. In theory, at least, nondiversified funds aim for the top of the performance charts, a perch that is hard to reach and nearly impossible to maintain. Funds that hit the top have a tendency to periodically hit rock bottom.

> A slim portfolio makes the fund more volatile than a sister fund holding the manager's top 100 picks—without any guarantee that long-term returns will be any better.

Nondiversified funds also defeat one of the primary purposes of investing in funds in the first place, namely, spreading out assets into more stocks than you could buy on your own. To that end, most experts suggest that nondiversified funds be treated like individual stocks or sector issues, accounting for no more than 25 percent of an average portfolio. As Michael Stolper of the San Diego investment advisory firm Stolper Asset Management notes: "These funds may be good, but you can't lose sight of the fact that they are appealing to our most basic emotion—greed. That doesn't make them bad funds, it's just that greed should not be a big factor in determining which type of fund you want to own."

THE LEAST YOU SHOULD REMEMBER

A diversified portfolio of mutual funds is built from many angles. You want to have a variety of assets and at least some representation of both growth and value investing.

One particular investment style may be most appealing to you—Don Phillips of Morningstar, for example, notes that he is a value investor at heart—but having both value and growth represented in a portfolio will smooth out performance every bit as much as diversifying between large- and small-company stocks.

Statistics show that investing your money in the stock market is nearly twice as secure as feeding it to otters.

—DAVE BARRY, *Miami Herald* HUMOR COLUMNIST

10

RISK

ON ANY GIVEN DAY, YOU WILL COME ACROSS products that claim to be fat free, guilt free, pain free, drug free, cholesterol free, or tax free.

But you will never find any investment that is risk free. It is unavoidable, the one and only completely sure thing in investing. In fact, avoiding one type of risk forces you to embrace another. Getting something—be it higher returns or more "safety"—means risking something. When you pursue higher returns, you are likely to buy a more volatile investment, with a greater chance of a decline. But when you pursue safety and put your money in government bonds, you run the risk that your money's growth will not keep up with the rate of inflation.

> Risk, in one form or another, is ever-present in the financial markets.

So, no matter what financial moves you make, you are awash in risk. The key is to avoid drowning in it, to understand it well enough to navigate your way through the risks and to a successful investment future. To do that, you may have to reshape the way you look at risk.

Most investors see risk only as the potential to lose money. Viewing risk through that incorrect lens is why, in nervous market times, many people try to eliminate risk by putting less money into stocks. But that move simply shifts and diversifies the risk, making it possible to avoid market downturns but not eliminating the risk altogether. If those investors simply turn their mattresses into piggy banks, they wipe out the risk of investment losses but maximize the risk that the money's buying power will be eaten away by inflation, not to mention the risk of losing the money to fire, burglary, or other potential threats.

As strange as it may seem, therefore, the best way to avoid risk may be to take on more of it—in different forms. Just consider the stocks-and-bonds equation, where bonds tend to be up when stocks are depressed. If all of your money is in stocks, you have no protection from a market downturn. If a sliver of your cash is invested in bonds, you will lose some of the market's growth potential, but your portfolio will do better when the market takes a dive. Overall, your portfolio should give a steadier ride.

> Owning investments that are not all subject to the same risks is an essential step in developing an investment portfolio that serves you well in all types of investment climate.

TYPES OF RISK

The key is to understand each type of risk and how certain investments fit together to make an all-weather portfolio. Here is a rundown on most of the risks faced by mutual-fund investors:

Shortfall risk.   Possibly the most overlooked form of risk of all, this has nothing to do with your actual investments and everything to do with your strategy. It is the potential for your investments to fall short of your goals, to leave you with a hole that you have no means of filling.

All too often, investors worry about losing money in the stock market but are so conservative that they can't make enough money to live out their days. Conversely, some people invest aggressively as if the goal is to make the most money; they make the needed amount, only to suffer a big loss that swallows enough of their nest egg to leave them wanting.

When it comes time to implement investment decisions, look carefully at the time horizon you have, along with any options you will have if you don't reach your goals. This will help you determine just how conservative or aggressive you can afford to be.

Market risk.   This is the risk that most of us fear—the possibility that a market crash or correction will wipe out an investment. But don't confuse market risk with volatility. The stock market, for instance, has been very volatile in the last decade, but it has not been particularly risky (and few people complain about volatility when the market is jolting ahead rather than stumbling).

Volatility—what happens in short-term swings—may determine whether an investment is too risky for you to own in the short term, but it works in both directions. If you want any investment that is going to provide above-average gains, you will need some volatility.

> Market risk is sometimes called principal risk.

Purchasing power risk.   Also called inflation risk, this is at the opposite end of the spectrum from market risk. It's the "risk of avoiding risk" that comes from being too conservative, meaning that the growth of your money does not keep pace with inflation.

Using the mattress example, someone sleeping on a nest egg is spending yesterday's dollars—what money was worth when the bed was stuffed—at today's prices. Someone who filled a mattress in the days of penny candy, for example, is not going to find life very sweet in today's more costly environment.

Interest-rate risk.   This double-edged risk, though it does affect fund investors, is more likely to impact people who buy bonds, certificates of deposit, and other conservative holdings. Say, for example, a consumer invests in a certificate of deposit. When the CD matures, the consumer risks not being able to invest at the same rate in the future. Conversely, people who tie up money in, say, long-term bonds, run the chance that interest rates will rise. Their locked-in return, in that circumstance, might not keep pace with inflation.

In funds, interest-rate changes can dramatically effect performance, for the good or the bad. Although bond funds are considered safe investments, a shaky interest-rate environment can make them more volatile than most people would expect.

> Market timing is trying to get out of the market just before a downturn or, conversely, getting in just before the market spikes.

Timing risk.   This has less to do with market timing than it does with your personal time horizon. Studies show, for example, that there has never been a twenty-year period when stocks have not made money. That means that if you have twenty years to invest, principal risk (the likelihood you will lose money) is low.

But stocks have lost money over any number of three-year periods. If your time horizon is three years, the likelihood that you could face a loss becomes much greater.

> The longer your time horizon, the easier it is to mitigate risk.

Liquidity risk. This takes several forms for mutual funds, most prominently in funds that trade in tiny market niches or developing nations. In those situations, if a fund faces a downturn and investors flee, the manager could be forced to sell stocks into a market where no one is buying. The results can be devastating.

Many observers fear that liquidity risk could be present among more commonplace stocks, too, but that it will not become evident until the market suffers a significant downturn and many fund managers are forced to meet redemptions at the same time.

> Several years ago a small fund called Van Eck Asia Infrastructure suffered a 16-percent loss in one day, all due to the fact that one major investor had decided to withdraw several million dollars.

Liquidity risk also takes the form of potential early withdrawal penalties or big tax bites that come with getting out of long-term investments before maturity. This lack of liquidity, coupled with the costs and the potential to need the money, should be considered before making the investment.

Property-appreciation risk. This is a phenomenon more common to real estate, collectibles, and tangible assets than funds, but it is worth understanding in the overall picture of risks that an investor takes.

Your biggest single investment may be your home. And you may have invested a ton of your disposable income in art, baseball cards, antique beverage containers, or any other collectible. But if the real-estate market takes a dive, the neighborhood deteriorates, or the world loses interest in, say, baseball cards, the investment can come up a loser and provide less profit than anticipated.

> There is no way any professor of economics or minister of the church can tell you what your risk tolerance should be.
> —**Paul Samuelson,**
> **Nobel Laureate in economics**

Property-appreciation risk also is closely tied to liquidity risk—no buyers for your home or your collection—and to timing risk, the need to sell at a time when the market is already flooded and prices are depressed.

Currency risk.   If you have a fund that invests heavily overseas and one of those countries suffers tremendous economic upheaval and has to devalue its currency, the value of your investments can drop like a stone. Not surprisingly, currency risk is often present wherever there is also political risk, which is the possibility that government actions—from simple elections escalating up to war—could radically alter the investment climate in a country. Although we see political risk in the United States, where the Republicans are considered more pro-business and good for the investment world than the Democrats, it is most often associated with foreign markets, where the stock markets are less developed and political upheaval can lead to outrageous volatility.

Credit risk.   This is the risk that the company or agency that owes your fund money—most likely a bond issuer—is going to fold or blow off its obligations. Although you might want to associate this issue solely with junk-bond funds, it can actually affect all types of bond funds. Consider the mid-1990s bankruptcy of Orange County, California, when many funds were left on the hook with bad debts.

> Junk-bond funds are also called "high-yield funds" because junk bonds must pay a good rate of interest to draw investors.

In most cases, the fund companies made up for their poor investments by bailing out their funds. Investors, therefore, did not lose a dime. But that kind of behavior is not guaranteed. Since the Orange County debacle, many money-market funds now carry insurance that will make good on bad debts. Still, the key for investors looking into bond funds is to make sure they understand the quality of the credit. The lower the ratings of the bonds purchased by the fund, the higher the credit risk for such debts if the fund is affected.

Dealing with all of these various types of risk requires looking at each investment individually and examining a worst-case scenario in real-dollar terms, as in: "How much will I lose if this investment blows up?"

You will quickly see that a portfolio that diversifies your types of risk trims the overall volatility of an investment portfolio. Combining market risk (stock investments) with purchasing-power risk (bonds, certificates of deposit) with property-appreciation risk (a home) and then adding other forms of risk, you are less vulnerable to any one catastrophe than if you keep all of your investments in one arena.

A MISTAKE TO AVOID

Many people fail to consider risk in real-dollar terms. Any fund that is capable of going up 20 percent in a year is equally capable of dropping by at least that much, so figure out how much a decline that large would cost you. If you have $10,000 invested, consider how a $2,000 loss would feel; if it makes you too nervous, consider whether you need to look at other types of funds.

Looking at a fund's downside potential in dollars, not percentages, encourages diversification, because you will be less likely to buy funds that will all take big declines in concert. This is particularly true as you get closer to retirement or to paying for college for your kids, when you may not want all of your portfolio subject to the kinds of large potential losses you were able to stomach as a young investor.

WRONG-WAY SIGNS

If your mutual funds all hold the same types of assets, you may have a diversified portfolio but you have not diversified your risks. Diversification is not about the number of funds you hold, but about the assets held by those funds.

The key in investing is to accept the risks you can accept and to try to avoid the risks that are too much for you.
—DICK WAGNER, A PRINCIPAL WITH THE DENVER FINANCIAL
FIRM SHARKEY, HOWES, WAGNER AND JAVER

TYPES OF FUNDS
NOT TO BUY

AS THE INTRODUCTION TO THIS BOOK EXPLAINED, there are no fund picks here. Simply put, a fund that's right for one investor isn't always good for another.

But it's a different story altogether when you start talking about bad mutual funds. A dog is a dog is a dog for everyone. The world's worst mutual funds, the Steadman Funds, had high costs and lousy performance, a combination that is good for no one.

And although there are good funds in every asset class, the truth is that there are some asset classes that investors are better off avoiding altogether. This list is highly personal. It reflects your risk tolerances and personal preferences, your ability to pick funds on your own, and other personal criteria.

My father, for example, cannot bring himself to buy small-cap funds. He likes being able to review a fund's portfolio and see names that he recognizes. Every time someone has analyzed his portfolio, they have come to the same conclusion: Dad is well-diversified except for owning small-company stocks. But no small-cap fund, whether it was picked by a financial adviser or by me, has ever passed my father's sniff test. He just can't pull the trigger on an investment that he really doesn't have faith or confidence in.

The result is a portfolio that has a hole in small caps but that has done sufficiently well in other areas so that it's not a concern. Sure, the lack of small-cap exposure might concentrate the risk and make the portfolio more volatile, but my father can sleep at night, knowing he has enough in assets and an investment time horizon to ride out a downturn.

Too many people believe that avoiding the wrong fund means sidestepping losers. That definition doesn't go far enough, because avoiding the wrong fund is also about keeping your money out of entire categories of funds that don't fit your mindset and methodology. Every type of mutual fund—and there are dozens of categories and more on the way—has its supporters and its own share of success stories. But some fund types, either by structure or the nature of the investment, are inefficient, redundant, too expensive, or downright inappropriate for you.

> That sleep factor—can you rest easy with your choices?—should be a big part of your investment strategy.

FUND TYPES TO CONSIDER AVOIDING

What all this is moving toward is a list of the types of funds that I would not buy for my own portfolio, followed by the reasons. The fund types that make this list didn't get here on the basis of performance; they simply do not meet my needs or desires. Just because a fund class shows up on my thumbs-down list is no reason for you to sell something that fits your strategy or has proven to you its ability to deliver. But if these fund classes are part of your portfolio— or if you would consider them for the future—you might want to examine other ways to pursue your investment goals. What's more, you should build your own list of fund types that will never pass your personal comfort test.

> Be aware that some global funds use "international" in their name, and vice versa. These are not comparable funds.

Here are the fund categories I tend to shun:

Global funds. If you want to invest your money abroad, be sure the boat leaves the dock. Global funds don't always weigh anchor. Unlike international funds—which buy only foreign issues—global funds throw U.S. shares in the pot. Some global funds are nearly 80-percent domestic, hardly the worldwide exposure that prompts most foreign investments.

For proof, check out the returns. In a year when the world markets are down and the U.S. market up—almost any year in the mid-1990s, for example—you will find that international funds lag global funds dramatically. That difference is entirely caused by global funds acting like domestic stock funds.

At the same time, the global funds did not actually return as much as true domestic stock funds. There's the rub.

International investing is an asset allocation, risk-spreading decision. If you choose to manage your money that way, make sure you get what you pay for; with a global fund, there is no guarantee.

Balanced funds.   There are plenty of terrific balanced funds out there, but they suffer from a malady similar to that of the global fund, which makes them inappropriate for many self-directed investors.

By rule, a balanced fund must keep at least 25 percent of its assets in stocks and 25 percent in bonds. The rest can swing either way, depending on the manager's judgment. As a result, bond funds are a common choice for newcomers to funds, people looking to get a mix of blue-chip stocks and high-grade bonds. But once you reach even a moderate level of sophistication, the balanced fund becomes obsolete in most portfolios.

As in global funds, where you can't control how much of your money is actually invested abroad, balanced funds can jump around; there's a big difference between having 75 percent of your holdings in stocks and having just 25 percent there.

Once an investor has decided to make asset allocation decisions personally, to pick how much money will be put in stocks and bonds, having some of it left in a fund that can go either way makes no sense to me. Furthermore, I dislike the fact that the average balanced fund has an expense ratio nearly equal to that of the average stock fund, which is curious because the big stake in bonds should make them much cheaper. In other words, you pay a lot and would still be better off picking individual funds that meet your stock- and bond-allocation needs.

Fund-of-funds, life-cycle funds, and asset-allocation funds.   These types of funds are designed to be one size fits all, and they are perfectly appropriate choices if all you want is one fund.

Truth be told, however, no one size fits everyone, and these funds generally don't fit well with a diversified fund investment strategy because—as with global and balanced funds—they don't exactly mesh with a personalized asset-allocation plan.

The fund-of-funds.   As the name implies, a fund-of-funds buys other mutual funds. This layers expenses—you pay costs for both the sponsor and the underlying funds—which cuts into performance. These funds come in different shapes and sizes—domestic, international, aggressive growth, and so on—but none are too attractive. As you will see later in this book, if the theory holds that owning too many funds makes a portfolio likely to act like an index fund, then a fund-of-funds is almost certain to perform like a costly index fund, and no one needs that.

A fund-of-funds is most appropriate as a default choice, as something for people with no interest in choosing and pursuing an investment strategy either in general or in a specific asset class. But if you are pursuing your own investment portfolio, you don't need this kind of fund structure.

The same can be said for life-cycle funds and asset-allocation funds. Life-cycle funds are designed to age as you do, so that the portfolio gets more conservative as you age, moving you from the stage where you need to grow your capital on into retirement, where you need to preserve it. Typically, the funds are age- or year-specific, targeted toward retirement at a certain point in the future.

> Both asset-allocation and life-cycle funds may be fine if you want to own only one fund. They stop being fine once you have more than one fund and try to do your own asset allocation.

One problem with these funds is that they assume you are average for your age. If you are more or less conservative, if you have higher retirement expectations and require more aggressive management, or if you have any number of other scenarios, these funds simply don't fit your life cycle.

Asset-allocation funds are similar, in that they try to pick a certain way to invest your assets so that you don't have to allocate them yourself. They often come in various flavors—growth, conservative, and the like—and they sometimes come in waves, where you start by investing in the fund family's aggressive allocation fund, then move your money toward the conservative allocation as you age.

> These funds, in reality, are not enhanced, nor are they index funds.

Enhanced index funds.   This is a simple concept: The Standard & Poor's 500 might deliver a good long-term return, but you could do even better if you dropped the ten or twenty worst stocks in the index and bought what was left.

The theory behind these funds doesn't work, because you don't get an index fund pegged to the remaining "Standard & Poor's 480"; you get an actively managed fund, complete with higher expenses and fraught with the same management foibles that drive true index-investors batty.

"Enhanced indexing" is a marketing gimmick. You'll be better off avoiding it.

Oddball index funds, and anything else based on a gimmick. Not every index is created equal. Take the Stock Car Stock Index, on which a successful mutual fund is based. The idea is that companies involved in the red-hot sport of auto racing make for good investments. But the number of companies that are actually involved in the races—building the cars and hitting the track—is tiny. So the index includes companies that sponsor race teams, which is to say, they buy advertising. (Think McDonald's here, or maybe Tide detergent, not Goodyear.)

That's no way to put together an index. And the same goes for many other new index products or new funds that are more packaging and promotion than sound investment idea.

Years ago, I had my cat pick stocks and created a yearlong index to see how her picks did. They beat the market. Today, someone would make a fund to track her picks. It would not be much different than the Wired Index—a high-tech index published by a magazine/on-line publishing company—or any other index that is not necessarily based on sound market principles.

> Unless you know what is going into the index, you can form no real expectation for the kind of performance that will come out of it.

Other gimmick funds include offerings like the dearly departed Pauze Tombstone, a fund that would be a sector fund covering the "death industry," except that there aren't enough funeral-home stocks to make a well-diversified fund. OpenFund started in 1999, with the big draw being that you had on-line access to management, through chat rooms and an open portfolio; that's all well and good, but it says nothing for the fund's investment strategy.

Bear-market, market-neutral, and other market-timing funds. Some funds are designed to make money when the market goes down. But since the market goes up, on average, two out of every three years, these funds are not likely to make money in the long term. These are not long-term investment vehicles; they are tools for timing the market.

Examine a fund like Rydex Ursa, which is designed to do exactly opposite what the Standard & Poor's 500 does. If the S&P were to go up 2,000-plus percent in the next two decades as it did in the last two decades, your investment would shrink to virtually zero. The same would happen in a variety of "ultrabull" and "ultrabear" funds, which try to supercharge market movements up or down. Think of an index fund on steroids (and where you pay a high fee for active management).

> Whenever a fund sells itself based on a hook—something catchy to grab you besides years of know-how and solid performance—you can bet that the fund is not worth owning.

In all cases, these funds tend to go feast-or-famine, topping the charts for one period and bringing up the rear the next. When they look good, the numbers are very enticing. The strategy, however, isn't good for anyone but the most sophisticated investors.

Market-neutral funds, designed to act like hedge funds, came into being a few years ago, when certain rules for funds were changed, and the market has been more negative than neutral to these offerings. They haven't proven their ability to make money in any market conditions, which is what a market-neutral strategy is supposed to do.

Ultimately, market timing is a loser's game. If you don't have a lot of confidence in your ability to call the direction of the stock market, don't even bother to look at these types of funds.

> Hedge funds are private pools of money available only to very wealthy investors.

Single-country and emerging-markets funds. Most investors can't stomach the flight of a sector fund, where assets are invested in one industry. But even sector investors should be leery of single-country offerings.

These funds have few investors and tend to buy illiquid issues, which makes for huge swings if they face big redemptions or if the country faces political or economic troubles. As a kicker, most single-country funds have high costs or commissions, or both; some have penalties for selling out in the first two years. About the only thing they guarantee is a bumpy ride.

Proponents of these funds would counter that they can offer eye-popping returns when things are good, and that's no lie. But it's worth noting that the

Lexington Troika Russia Fund proved in the late 1990s that it was perfectly capable of racking up big numbers on the plus and minus side of the ledger, earning a huge return one year, only to give most of it back the next.

If some of my money is going overseas, I want it in a diversified fund in markets that do not remind me of the Wild Wild West. Anything that is less diversified than that or that invests in the stock markets of nations like Ghana is just not for me.

Internet funds.   A child of the late 1990s, this subset of the fund world started with just a few offerings. Then by the start of 2000, seemingly every fund company either had considered or had opened an Internet fund to capitalize on the success of the first few. That statistic notwithstanding, my reasons for not wanting an Internet fund have to do with the fact that I can't be quite sure what one is.

Some of these funds want to invest mostly in computer and networking companies, investing in the technology stocks involved in building the infrastructure for the Internet. Others are buying companies that do business over the Internet, including traditional retailers like The Gap or Office Depot that have simply developed a big presence on the World Wide Web.

By that definition, virtually any company in existence today might qualify as an Internet stock, the same way that McDonald's qualifies as a "stock car stock," merely by association.

That's not a strong enough link for me.

There are plenty of funds with significant assets tied up in Internet stocks—regardless of how those stocks are defined—that could provide me with that kind of exposure.

For now, I can't see anything consistent from one Internet fund to the next, hence I can't get a

> Although the Internet is no gimmick and funds that concentrate on one industry can be viable, my feelings are that I don't have to rush to the end of the risk scale to improve my returns.

good read on the strategy. The science-and-technology sector funds have a longer record, and they load up on Internet stocks that lean toward technology development rather than retailing and have a more clearly defined mission. Until I can say the same about Internet funds—or any new type of fund that comes down the pike—I will not invest in that asset class.

Given how quickly the Internet world is evolving, however, my feelings for this type of fund could change in time. After all, the last part of making up a no-buy list of funds is reserving the right to change your mind.

THE RIGHT WAY TO PROCEED

Make a list of funds that you do not think belong in your portfolio—these are the ones that would not be right for you based on what they buy or how they invest. In doing so, you will be weeding out a large segment of the fund world.

If you are a young, aggressive investor, you might rule out bond funds. If you are an older, conservative investor, it could be aggressive-growth funds or small-cap funds (like my Dad) that you reject. Your list should be based on your own preferences, not necessarily on market science. You do not need to own one of each type of fund—you need to own only those types of funds that you think will allow you to sleep at night and still reach your goals.

Combine this list with a list of the traits you consider important in a fund, and you will be able to screen out a huge number of funds that will never be right for you.

LOAD VERSUS NO-LOAD

TO MANY PEOPLE, "LOAD" IS THE DIRTIEST four-letter word in investing.

It seems obvious that given their druthers, no one would actually want to pay a load when they don't actually have to. But the truth isn't quite so simple.

The load-versus-no-load debate reaches all the way back into the 1920s, the earliest days of the fund business. For roughly the first sixty years of mutual funds, it was a straightforward debate, too. Sales loads, during those times, were essentially front-end commissions. If you invested $1,000, a few percentage points' worth of that money would go into the pocket of the salesman rather than into your account. That difference alone was, in the minds of many consumers, enough to make no-load funds the superior product, simply because putting all of your money to work was intuitively better than losing a shred of that money forever.

> A load is a sales charge, generally paid to an adviser selling a fund.

As a result, the fund industry developed new ways to charge customers for the services of an adviser. The result was loaded funds that looked like they carried no sales charge.

Again, the public reacted as if these funds—most of which merely cloned an existing fund but used a different pricing structure—somehow became better performers because they didn't carry a visible sales charge. That kind of thinking—which many investors still harbor—is both anachronistic and wrong.

These days, you can avoid loads—or sales charges—on some load funds and pay advisory fees for a portfolio of no-load funds.

Mark Riepe, head of the Schwab Center for Investment Research in San Francisco, notes that there aren't even any disreputable studies—ones investors would be foolish to believe—saying that either load or no-load funds actually have a performance advantage. "Loads are about distribution, not returns," Riepe says. "Managers don't care whether their fund is load or no-load. That's for the sales staff to worry about. The load structure—or lack thereof—should not affect how the fund is run in the least."

> Moreover, studies have shown that many factors determine a fund's long-term superiority and that loads are not necessarily one of them.

In short, people who believe that no-load funds *must* be good and loads *must* be bad have taken their eye off the ball.

"People worry more about the way they pay for a fund than about either how much they pay for the fund or what they get for their money," says Don Phillips, president of Morningstar, Inc. "If you focus in on one piece of the puzzle, you may never figure out what the big picture really looks like."

Today, the real issue revolves less around sales charges than it does around expenses. The terms "load" and "no-load" are virtually meaningless. Funds can charge fees up front, on redemption and—using the 12b-1 fee—over the entire period you own a fund. Even no-load funds can charge a small 12b-1 fee—despite the fact that they don't have advisers doing sales and marketing—without forfeiting their legal status as a "no-load" fund.

> The 12b-1 fee goes to sales and marketing costs.

Load funds are often sold without fees, such as in retirement plans or in the no-transaction-fee mutual-fund supermarket systems. The supermarket systems, in turn, created a way for advisers to manage clients' money in the best available funds, regardless of sales loads. The advisers get paid a portion of the money they manage; it's not a load, but you pay it regardless of whether the adviser buys load or no-load funds.

Yes, loads are a drag on performance, but no more so than high expenses.

For proof that one side does not dominate the other when it comes to performance, simply look at the charts. No-load funds may not have a sales charge, but that doesn't always result in better performance. In fact, the top gainers over time appear to be pretty well split between funds with and without sales charges.

If load funds, on average, are likely to provide the same returns as no-load funds during any given period—as shown in several studies—the choice comes down to "do it yourself" or "hire some help."

If you need help, go out and get it, but pay for it in the fashion that you find most fair. Some people like old-fashioned up-front loads, others don't want to feel like they are paying a commission. Choose the means of paying for help that most suits you, but be certain to look at the total cost of ownership rather than just the cost of the load.

> There are two real issues that you need to sort out in considering load and no-load funds.
> 1. **Help versus no help**
> 2. **Total cost of ownership**

Let's examine the cost structure of two popular, successful funds and see what's behind the costs:

As this book went to press, Guardian Park Avenue A charged a 4.5-percent sales load and a tiny 12b-1 fee, plus an expense ratio of 0.79 percent. Wasatch Growth Fund was a pure no-load fund with an expense ratio of 1.5 percent, just below the average growth fund according to Lipper, Inc.

> "No-load" does not necessarily mean "low-cost"; that is, a load fund with low expenses can sometimes be cheaper to own than an average no-load fund. That's why investors should look at all charges and not just sales loads.

Looking at their prospectuses, you learn that if both funds earned a 5-percent return over ten years, your cost of ownership per $1,000 invested—including expenses plus applicable sales charges—would be $181 for the Wasatch fund, compared to $167 for Guardian Park Avenue. Hold the fund longer and the gap grows. And although both funds have significantly topped that 5-percent return mark, Guardian's cost advantage grows even wider if it outperforms Wasatch, which it has over the last decade.

Of course, examples can be constructed in many ways. It is just as easy to show a low-cost no-load fund that outperforms a fund with a sales charge on both an expense and performance basis.

But if you can buy a load fund without paying the sales charge—in a retirement account or through a fund supermarket—it becomes a de facto no-load fund. More important, you have lowered the fund's cost of ownership.

Likewise, adding an adviser's annual management fee to the costs of a no-load fund creates an additional drag on performance.

With that in mind, let's examine the cost structure of paying for advice and see how various types of sales charges are levied and how it affects you.

> Funds that offer the best deal will match your need for help with a reasonable cost structure, all wrapped into a fund whose mission and objective you believe in.

CLASSIFIED SHARES

Fund companies cooked up alphabet soup to appease investors who didn't want to pay up-front charges on traditional advisor-sold funds. Here's how you should think of the different types of shares.

Think of *Class A* shares as meaning "all at once." This is the standard, one-shot, front-end load share, and most often, a long-term investor will find that simple and old-fashioned works. If you plan to hold almost any load fund for six or more years, there's a very good chance that the Class A shares will have the lowest ownership costs over time.

Class B stands for "back-end load," meaning these shares carry a charge that is payable if the fund is sold within four to six years. The load typically declines the longer the fund is held, until it disappears. But for as long as the load is in place, Class B shares carry a heightened expense ratio (making up for the missed load). That raises costs until the redemption period expires, when most B shares convert to lower-expense A shares.

If you are looking at Class B shares, make sure they have that conversion feature. Without it, you are certain to come up a loser on costs compared to A shares over time.

Consistency is what *Class C* shares are about. Sometimes called "level-load" shares—although they have neither a front- or back-end sales charge—Class C issues have higher expenses for as long as you own the fund, making this an expensive way to own a long-term holding.

Class M shares can best be summed up as being "middle of the road," a compromise between the other share types. M shares carry a smaller front-end load than A shares, and a smaller 12b-1 fee than B and C shares.

Class Y shares, in general, are for institutional investors and fund-company employees, and they typically come with the load stripped off or the fees trimmed down. The catch is that the buy-in point is high, requiring the kind of money a bank has lying around rather than your spare investment dollars. In this case, you might as well think of the Y as standing for "you can't afford this." That said, however, if you have really big dollars to invest—at least

$100,000 in a single account—you should at least inquire as to whether you can get a pricing bargain and buy Y shares if they are available.

In addition to the common share classes, fund companies are always dreaming up new payment forms and coming up with their own name for it, whether it goes by a letter or under some moniker like "advisor class shares" (which can only be sold through a financial intermediary). A number of fund companies are hoping to be allowed to issue E shares, which would essentially carry a lower expense ratio but would require the investor to interact with the fund company entirely over the Internet, instead of by U.S. mail.

No matter what kind of shares the fund business dreams up next, the rule is "follow the money" and compare the costs. When it comes to sales charges and fees, the numbers never lie.

SALES AND MARKETING (12B-1) FEES

A 12b-1 fee functions like an annual load, often of as much as 1 percent. Some of the money goes to the fund, some to your adviser. All of it raises your cost of ownership. Technically, however, a 12b-1 fee is not a load. In fact, a fund can charge a sales or marketing fee of up to 0.25 percent and still call itself "no-load."

But don't ignore this charge, especially since this is where the Class B and Class C shares hide the extra charges that you pay *instead* of a load.

SHORT-TERM REDEMPTION FEES

Some funds, particularly those in narrowly traded asset classes, charge investors who pull out soon after buying in. It smells like a back-end load, but isn't. For starters, expenses are unaffected. Moreover, the fee pays a fund's costs in a quick turnaround, reducing the need to liquidate hard-to-sell holdings. In other words, it protects shareholders who stick around and hurts those who don't, so don't let this kind of fee turn you off to a fund.

TRANSACTION FEES

These little-known beauties feel like an up-front load, but aren't. Collected mostly on index funds by a few companies, these fees cover the cost of investing your money. At Vanguard Group, the company using transaction fees most widely, they range from 0.25 percent to 1 percent on selected funds.

You pay this money even without transaction fees; you just have no idea of the cost because a fund's trading costs are not part of its expense ratio. Instead, brokerage fees are simply taken off the top of a fund's returns, before other expenses are applied.

WRAP ACCOUNT OR ADVISORY FEES

If you buy no-load funds but pay for help selecting and managing them, consider your adviser's fee a load. Technically it isn't, but it clearly effects the cost of ownership. Besides, depending on your investment personality, you may pay more in advisory fees than you ever would in straight commission sales charges.

> Transaction fees aren't loads because they pay only the cost of putting the money to work.

If you are the kind of person who wants an adviser to help you pick funds that you plan to hold forever, the cost of an up-front sales charge will be a lot less than a lifetime's worth of advisory fees paid on a fund you have no intention of ever selling.

Michael Stolper of the San Diego–based advisory firm Stolper Asset Management says: "Pick the best funds available first, then worry about the sales charges and costs. Investing is not about whether you paid a sales charge, it's about how much money you have when you need it. If you are no good at picking funds yourself, saving on a load is not going to make you money in the end."

THE LEAST YOU SHOULD REMEMBER

It's not how you get charged, it's how much. Funds and investment advisers have a lot of ways to skin your account beyond the classic, up-front straight commission. If something affects your account, factor the total cost into the equation and see which structure is best for you.

THE RIGHT WAY TO PROCEED

If you are paying for financial help and considering mutual funds that have share classes, make your adviser show you how much—in real dollars—you will pay if you buy the A, B, C, or M shares. If they aren't picking the share type with the lowest costs over the number of years you expect to own the fund, demand an explanation.

It's one thing to pay for help when you need it; it's completely different to get fleeced by someone who wants to make every possible dollar off you.

EXPENSE RATIOS

PEOPLE CELEBRATE OR BEMOAN PERFORMANCE, but the most critical underpinning of how the fund will do actually can be found in its *expense ratio: The total costs shareholders pay annually to cover the fund's operating costs and management fees*. The expense ratio includes 12b-1 fees, which are supposed to pay for sales and marketing of the fund.

As this book was being written, Lipper, Inc. pegged the average expense ratio for a stock fund at just over 1.6 percent, or $16 per year for every $1,000 you have in a fund account. The average expense ratio on bond funds was just under 1.1 percent. This is one of the great drawbacks of mutual funds. If you buy stocks, you pay the trading costs to make the purchase, but you have no ongoing costs of ownership.

> A fund's expense ratio is equal to taking its total operating expenses on an annualized basis divided by its assets. The higher the expense ratio, the more you pay to the fund company in fees.

With funds, however, you pay a piece of your money to the fund's operators every day. Expenses are deducted regularly, before share prices are updated each day. Calculated that way, they are so small that you don't feel them. Over time, however, those little slivers of your holdings add up and have a surprisingly large impact on the growth of your holdings.

Expenses amount to the fund's management fee and most associated costs. They include the 12b-1 fee, which is supposed to be a sales and marketing fee but which often acts as a means of flattening out a sales charge. It is important to note that the expense ratio does not include the fund's trading costs. You pay those, too, which means that a fund with high turnover may have additional "friction costs" beyond the mere expense ratio that can dampen your return.

Typically, expenses vary based on the size of the fund and the cost controls of management. Expenses are independent of sales charges, so every fund—even "no-load" funds that do not charge a sales fee—takes its cut of assets to pay for manager salaries, shareholder services, administration, and other expenses. That cut comes right off the top.

So let's say a fund with a 1.0-percent expense ratio invests in stocks that generate a 10-percent return over the course of the year. Your return investing in that fund would amount to 9 percent, or the amount generated by the fund's investments minus the amount you paid management.

The expense is the "friction" that scrapes away some of your return as the fund moves forward. It would seem obvious, therefore, that lower costs result in better performance. That certainly is true when comparing one index fund with another, if both funds mimic the same benchmark and any discrepancy in return is almost certainly attributable to different costs. But it doesn't always work out that way when looking at actively managed funds where one might make better investments that overcome the higher costs.

> Performance, of course, comes with no guarantees that it will continue. Expenses, however, are pretty much a sure thing.

When a fund can deliver bigger gains that outweigh the heightened costs of a heavy expense ratio, investors won't complain. It's only when returns suffer that shareholders complain about how much the management company takes for expenses, figuring that they have overpaid for poor performance.

When it comes to a mutual fund's expense ratio, *you are looking for quality that exceeds the cost*. You get that either by getting great performance or by investing in low-cost funds where the performance bar does not have to be set so high in order to succeed.

Although a fund may peg a portion of the costs on performance—so that you pay more than a base amount only if the fund racks up superior performance—the norm is that you can examine a fund's expense ratio today and expect the numbers to stay in the same neighborhood in the future.

And though it is easy to overlook a 2-percent expense ratio when a fund is gaining 20 percent per year, you need to consider what happens if the fund's performance falters. The same 2 percent is going to look mighty greedy in a year when it eats half of your gains or, worse yet, you lose money.

As Bill Berger, the late founder of the Berger Funds and a pioneer of fund investing once told me: "If you pick the wrong fund manager—someone who can't consistently give you the kind of returns you want—you can't blame that one on the fees. It is the investor's job to determine whether they will get their money's worth from the management company, no matter what they are paying."

> For more on performance, see Section 15.

Obviously, expenses should be a key decision point in the purchase of a fund and often are a valuable tiebreaker for picking between two good funds.

In examining expenses, compare a fund's ratio to both industry averages and peers. Some classes of funds—international and emerging markets funds, for example—carry costs that are much higher than the typical stock fund just to make up for the research costs of building a portfolio in faraway lands. If you want that type of fund in your portfolio, measure its expenses mostly against peers, to see if it is in line with the competition. Size it up against the average just to make sure that you believe the heightened costs are actually worth it.

> The fund with the lower costs gets the nod whenever you try to choose between two similar funds.

You can find expense data and the long-term costs of ownership in the first two pages of most funds' prospectus. There you will find a table that shows, in absolute dollars, how much you will pay to own a fund, based on a 5-percent average rate of return. What's not so obvious in those charts is that because expense ratios represent a percentage of assets, the more money you have invested, the more you pay in absolute dollars.

So here is some easy math to help you.

If you invest in a fund that returns 10 percent *before expenses* for ten years,

> Remember, too, that expenses are particularly crucial in bond funds, where the market generally keeps returns within a certain range and the top and bottom performers tend to be separated by an amount equal to the difference between their costs.

every 0.25 in expense ratio will cost you roughly $55 per $1,000 you have invested. Divide the expense ratio on any fund you are considering by 0.25, then multiply the result by $55 to get a loose approximation of what to expect in costs per $1,000 invested if your fund delivers a 10-percent return.

So, if you invest $10,000 in a fund with a 1.0-percent expense ratio and that fund delivers an annualized average gain of 10 percent for the next decade, at the end of those ten years, you will have paid the fund in excess of $2,200. Your real return would be 9 percent after expenses.

By comparison, if the fund charged just 0.25 percent in expenses, your cost over ten years would be just over $550. That difference—indeed the entire $2,200-plus—may not feel like much, as your $10,000 investment would have more than doubled over that time period. But it adds up. In the low-cost fund, your account would end the decade with about $25,350, or roughly $1,750 more than in the high-cost fund.

When you look at the raw-dollar figures that way—and that's with a fund that was a winner—it's easy to see why any fund charging above-average expenses requires enough investigation to feel sure that you are paying for—and can expect to get—superior management. You'd rather own a great fund with a high expense ratio than a mediocre performer with lower costs, but don't pay above-average expenses unless you are confident of getting above-average returns.

THE RIGHT WAY TO PROCEED

Download SEC's Mutual Fund Cost Calculator for free at **www.sec.gov**. Developed by the agency, the program eliminates much of the mystery in fund math. You plug in an investment amount, the expected holding period, the fund's total expense ratio, up-front or deferred sales loads, and your anticipated rate of return.

A few clicks later, the software provides the total cost of holding a fund for the specified time period, assuming that growth meets your expectations. The cost figure includes fees paid, plus any earnings you lose as a result of those fees. In short, this tool will allow you to run a free cost comparison on the funds you are considering for your portfolio.

It's not perfect. A fund that experiences volatile performance, for example, would produce costs much different than the SEC program's straight-line average gain. The real numbers could be better or worse than projected. That said, the program is a vast improvement over the typical disclosures a fund makes in its prospectus.

THE LEAST YOU SHOULD REMEMBER

Lower costs do not necessarily lead to superior performance. But since fund fees don't usually go down, a low-cost fund has a smaller hill to climb to deliver positive returns.

> *If you pay the executives at Sara Lee more, it doesn't make the cheesecake less good. But with mutual funds, it comes directly out of the batter.*
>
> —Don Phillips, president of Morningstar, Inc.

> The mutual-fund prospectus is explained in detail in Section 34.

TURNOVER

A FEW YEARS AGO, A FUND MANAGER CALLED ME on a Monday to say he was coming to town and wanted to meet for lunch on Wednesday. He had a good track record but a reputation for churning his portfolio and changing his mind rather frequently. After we arranged the meeting, I asked him about his favorite current stock.

On Tuesday, he called to shift the time of our lunch. Before we hung up, he volunteered that he had a new favorite stock.

At lunch on Wednesday, he confided that there was a new favorite and that he had sold out of the position he was so in love with on Monday.

On Thursday, he called to get my fax number to send along some follow-up information. You guessed it, he also had a new favorite stock.

Some fund managers change their portfolio more often than they change their socks. Since you probably won't be invited to lunch by your fund's managers, you will have to look at their "turnover ratio" to see who is a trader and who is a buy-and-holder.

Turnover refers to how often managers buy and sell the average stock in their portfolio. A turnover ratio of 100 percent, therefore, implies that the manager turns over the entire portfolio—selling everything and replacing it all with something new—once a year. Since these transactions can generate trading costs and can result in taxable gains, turnover is a number that has meaning to you, the shareholder. Unfortunately, it frequently means very little to the fund manager.

The fund manager I had my lunch with was unapologetic for his trading frequency. In fact, with the average stock fund having an average turnover rate of more than 75 percent, it's obvious that the majority of managers are more focused on year-end (or worse yet, quarterly) gains than they are on how turnover is impacting the performance.

Whenever a fund manager sells a security at a profit, you pick up a capital gains exposure. If you hold the fund in a retirement account, this is no big deal. But if the fund is in a taxable account and the gain is not offset by some loss, that gain is going to cost you. On a federal level, if the fund held the stock for more than a year, 20 percent of your gain goes to Uncle Sam. If the stock was a quick-hit turnaround and was held for less than a year, you get taxed at your regular income-tax rate, which can be nearly 40 percent. What's worse, you can get hit with these gains even when the fund is losing money or falling behind its peers. Perhaps the most famous example of this occurred in 1997, when Foster Freiss of the Brandywine Fund made an ill-timed decision to move from stocks to cash; he sold his winners and generated a huge taxable gain for shareholders, while losing 7 percent in December alone.

> Turnover statistics are part of the "financial history" numbers in a fund's prospectus, and they can be telling.

Turnover doesn't just affect a fund's tax efficiency, it also impacts the overall expense ratio. Several studies have shown that high-turnover funds tend to be more expensive; remember, too, that those expense ratios *do not* include the actual trading costs. Add those costs in, and the fund's friction costs go up even further.

Buy-and-hold strategies typically would be characterized by turnover ratios of 30 percent or less, while anything above 100 percent reflects some serious trading. Yet some buy-and-hold managers have higher turnover because they quickly cut losers from the margins of their portfolio while searching for something good to add to their long-term portfolio; they hold their core stocks for ages, but on paper, they look as if they are moving money willy-nilly.

"The impact of turnover is tough to gauge because some low-turnover managers are superstars and others are slugs," says Robert Markman of the Markman MultiFunds, which invest in other mutual funds. "Likewise, some high-turnover managers are hopped-up day traders, others are superstars."

In short, turnover numbers are not predictive—they can't help show you which fund is going to do well going forward. But there have been any number of studies that have shown that high-turnover strategies place more emphasis on the skill of the manager.

It's not surprising, therefore, that index funds have very low turnover rates.

As a result, think of a fund manager as a race-car driver, and look at turnover numbers as a measure of driving activity. The turnover statistics suggest whether your driver is driving a constant steady line or weaving through traffic in a rough-but-fast course.

You need to decide which kind of driver you want for your money.

TURNOVER CONSIDERATIONS

When reviewing turnover statistics, be certain to consider:

Turnover compared to peers. Certain asset classes tend to foster more turnover, which is fine so long as the fund is consistent with its investment objective. The average growth-and-income fund, for example, has a turnover rate of roughly 65 percent; a growth-and-income fund with turnover beyond 100 percent, therefore, is acting more like an aggressive, small-stock fund rather than the kind of growth-and-income offering you might expect.

By comparison, in some volatile sectors and markets, quick hits are common and turnover tends to be higher. A 75-percent turnover rate, for example, is above average for growth-and-income funds but well below average for technology sector funds. If turnover is out of line with the competition, the fund may not be run in a fashion that is consistent with your expectations.

Consistency. If a fund's turnover remains constant, management has likely not changed its style. If turnover jumps—particularly if performance falters—you have a sign that the manager is casting about, foundering and desperately trying to figure out what to do next.

If you are thinking of buying a fund that has a good long-term record but has lagged recently and shown a big increase in its turnover, you may want to put off the purchase to see whether things stabilize. You don't want to buy a fund when big changes may be afoot.

Tax implications. A high-turnover fund typically generates a bigger annual capital-gains payout, which means a higher current tax bill. A buy-and-hold fund puts off most of its gains and reduces your current tax bill.

If high-turnover funds grab your attention, consider limiting them to your retirement plans and other tax-deferred accounts and stick with the more tax-efficient, low-turnover funds for monies on which you will have to pay any current-gains taxes.

> Studies show that funds with average to low turnover post better after-tax returns than faster-trading counterparts.

Potential impact on performance. High turnover coupled with above-average expenses should make you nervous, yet it's quite common. All of the research that goes into a frenetic trading pace has to be paid for somehow, and you are the one who is likely to foot the bill.

The manager will need to generate returns big enough to pay for all of those costs and still keep returns attractive. That's hard to do consistently when trading and expenses take a deeper-than-average cut into returns.

The reason for the turnover. As the owner of a mutual fund, you have a right to know why the manager makes so many moves and exposes you to a strategy that could cost you some dollars in after-tax returns. It may be that the manager follows a certain investment style or system. It may be that the manager makes big sector bets and is constantly moving the fund into and out of different market segments.

Whatever the reason, make sure it makes sense to you and that you believe in it. If not, chances are that you can find a low-turnover alternative that is just as suitable for your money and that does not saddle you with the burden of the manager's helter-skelter maneuvering.

THE LEAST YOU SHOULD REMEMBER

High-turnover funds tend to be most efficient in tax-deferred accounts, where capital gains thrown off during trading don't hurt you. If you are buying a fund for a taxable account, turnover rate may help you decide between two choices.

It doesn't show which fund will perform better, but it does give you a hint about which fund may present you with the lower tax burden in the future.

> *Average investors who try to do a lot of trading will just make their brokers rich.*
>
> —HARVARD UNIVERSITY FINANCE
> PROFESSOR MICHAEL JENSEN

15

WHAT PAST PERFORMANCE **REALLY** SAYS ABOUT A FUND

WHEN A MUTUAL FUND TOUTS its results in an advertisement, it includes a disclaimer that *past performance is no indicator of future returns*. But most investors blow past that danger sign the way a smoker ignores the surgeon general's warning. As with cigarettes, however, the warning is there for a reason: Failing to heed this danger sign could be hazardous to your wealth.

The problem with past performance is that you don't live in the past. If you drove down the highway looking entirely into the rearview mirror, sooner or later you would crash. Past performance numbers are a fund's rearview mirror.

> No matter how good a fund has been over time, it is only as good for you as the returns it racks up while you own it.

In 1999, a Financial Research Corporation study showed that the top 10 percent of funds in any twelve-month period since 1988 dropped, on average, to the forty-eighth percentile during the following year. Roughly half of the time, those funds were below-average performers within a year of scaling the fund summit.

At the same time, roughly 40 percent of the worst performers in any given year put up above-average gains during the twelve months after bottoming out. In other words, funds tend to regress toward average performance, which is a big reason to consider carefully whether you want to jump into any fund trumpeting its recent gains.

Plenty of other studies have confirmed this kind of data. Worse yet, investors tend to get the wrong side of that performance. The same Financial Research Corporation study showed that top-selling funds—the very ones that presumably attract the most money because they have had superior performance—wind up delivering below-average results going forward. Some of this problem may stem from having to put all that new cash to work. According to the study, the top-selling funds tend to be below-average performers in the year after raking in the dough.

That's why Securities and Exchange Commission chairman Arthur Levitt has warned investors against putting too much stock in past performance. That is the reason, as this book has already suggested, you must look at costs, turnover, volatility, investment objective, and all of the other factors that make a fund a good purchase.

> The performance numbers you see in a fund's advertising can dramatically overstate what you are likely to get once you buy the fund.

That said, past performance still plays a big role in your decision to buy a fund. You want to buy a fund that can inspire your confidence, and that's not going to happen in a fund without a proven record of producing decent returns.

The key is to not fall in love with a fund's past, to see numbers in an advertisement and assume that your money will grow at that rate in the future. If past performance is going to be a useful part of your fund-selection process, you need to look beyond the raw performance numbers.

ASSESSING A FUND'S PERFORMANCE RECORD

Here is what you need to know about a fund's past glories:

1. How was this performance accomplished?   The numbers tell a story about a fund, but it's the Cliff Notes version. All of the fine details have been cut out, boiled down to a conclusion. Your job is to do the detective work.

Simply put, you want to know the story behind the fund. Most funds have a compelling reason for their success or failure. It has to do with their strategy, what they look for in stocks, or how they do their research. The more dramatically a fund beats the competition, the more important it is to figure out what's driving the success.

It could simply be that the fund invests in the hot asset class, in which case performance is likely to cool when some other type of investment comes into favor. It also could be that the fund was small and was able to benefit from its size. It might be that the fund profited from a simple strategy like indexing or concentrating the portfolio.

> If a fund can't explain the key to its success, it probably doesn't know how to continue that success. It may just have gotten lucky.

A tiny fund, for example, needs to pick only one or two winners—or to get a small number of shares in a hot initial public offering—to post big gains. When the cash then rolls in, the fund can't get enough of those IPO shares or a big enough stake in tiny undiscovered stocks to maintain the pace of gains it started out with.

2. Was the current manager in place throughout the attractive performance period?   If most of a fund's success came at the direction of a former manager, it could be a sign of trouble for the fund today. Make sure you know how much of the great performance occurred on the current manager's watch. If new management hasn't been around long enough to let you determine that the fund is likely to keep returns above average, the past performance numbers are useless.

3. How does performance vary over different time periods?   A performance ad will tell you that a fund was the top-ranked fund over a year or a decade. It seldom tells you how the fund did in each of those years—yet that piece of information is crucial.

A few years ago, I studied ten years of quarterly performance for growth and capital-appreciation funds (today, most people would consider "capital-appreciation" funds to be "aggressive-growth" funds). PBHG Growth, the top-ranked capital appreciation fund over the ten years, ranked among the top ten funds of its peers in fourteen separate quarters. It also had five quarters among the absolute dregs of its peer group. Meanwhile, Fidelity Contrafund, the top-ranked growth fund for the entire period, suffered one quarter at the bottom of its peer group but didn't crack the top ten for a single quarter.

Obviously, one fund was streaky, the other steady. Both approaches were long-term winners for investors who stayed buckled up for the full ten-year ride.

If you only look at long-term performance numbers, you don't get a sense of the ups and downs the fund has the potential to put you through.

4. What is the performance downside? This is an extension of the last question, where you turn past performance on its ear. To do this, evaluate quarterly returns over several years. Presumably, you can ride out the ups, so focus on the downs, plugging your numbers into the worst the fund has dished out. Turn the fund's worst quarter into a decimal (a 20-percent loss equals .2, for example) and multiply it by the amount you plan to invest. The result is the kind of three-month paper loss the fund is capable of inflicting upon you.

Now repeat the process a few times—multiplying your remaining money by the fund's worst quarter and adding it to your first loss—to see what happens over six months, then nine months, then a year.

Another alternative is to simply take the fund's best period of performance and turn it upside down, because any fund capable of generating big gains can also produce big losses. If the numbers make you sweat, look for another fund.

5. How does that performance compare to similar funds? Any fund can look good in a vacuum. The question is how the fund performs relative to similar funds and to relevant benchmarks. Remember, it's entirely possible for a fund to produce great absolute results but to not look so good when compared to peers. During the bull market of the late 1990s, for instance, many large-company growth funds were putting up 15-percent annualized average gains that looked terrific until compared to the S&P 500's bigger returns and the average gains of the competition.

> Every fund shows performance in its prospectus, benchmarked against either the appropriate index or the Lipper, Inc. average performance for its fund type.

6. What is management saying you can expect from future performance? Ironically, what a fund company says in its advertisement is "Look at our fantastic results!" But what it says in statements to shareholders is "We're happy to have been able to produce great results for you last year, but you should not necessarily expect that performance to continue."

Nevertheless, managers tend to be forthcoming with the reasons behind their expectations for future performance. When requesting information on a fund, then, make sure they send you not only the prospectus but also the two most recent semiannual reports, plus any newsletters or other correspondence the fund or the manager has sent shareholders. Remember, you become one of those shareholders the moment you buy the fund; you are entitled to see what kind of materials those owners have been getting that would shape their expectations.

Ultimately, your goal is likely to be a fund with an above-average history that tends to do reasonably well in all market conditions and that offers steadiness of performance rather than marked highs and lows. Remember: Don't be sucked in based mostly on past performance. It was good news only for the people who owned the fund in the past.

> Read the manager's statements carefully. It will tell you a lot more than the marketing department could stick into an ad.

SOMETHING TO CONSIDER

Mark Hulbert, editor of the *Hulbert Financial Digest,* a newsletter that tracks the performance of investment newsletters, has done outstanding research on persistence of performance. In one such study, Hulbert compared a portfolio of "market beaters"—managers who beat the market over the previous twelve months—to "market laggards" who had trailed the market during the previous year.

Over fifteen years, the market beaters' portfolio earned a 99-percent return, which seems good until you consider that the laggards earned 350 percent over the same time period. During the same fifteen years studied, however, the Wilshire 5000 Index—designed to represent the "total stock market"—was up over 600 percent.

A MISTAKE TO AVOID

If you find yourself ready to purchase a fund that is listed at the very top of the quarterly or annual performance charts, you are timing the market, not making a long-term fund investment. Invariably, funds that reach the absolute top of the heap for a short period were buoyed by some sort of right-place, right-time luck. Most often, these funds focus on specific industries or regions, which could turn out to be the wrong place in a big hurry.

The bottom of those same performance charts is almost always littered with similar funds that focused on out-of-favor sectors and businesses. When the market turns, you could go from the top to the bottom of the charts in a hurry.

RATINGS VERSUS RANKINGS

IF YOU CAN'T PICK A FUND BASED ON THE STRENGTH of its past performance, then the next best thing would be to pick it based on its ratings, the observation of some independent third-party observer. After all, it works in hotels and restaurants, where you can be almost universally assured that a four- or five-star establishment is going to be worth your money.

Clearly, this kind of thinking has gripped fund investors since the mid-1990s, when Morningstar ratings became a key part of the lexicon of fund investors. Since then, virtually every dollar flowing into mutual funds has gone into those issues carrying Morningstar's four-and five-star ratings.

Although firms like Morningstar and Value Line provide a valuable service, they have limits that are important to understand when you pick a fund.

But first, let's examine the difference between ratings and rankings.

RANKINGS ARE PURE PERFORMANCE

These are the numbers—most widely quoted from sources like Lipper, Inc. or CDA Wiesenberger—that compare a fund's total return to that of its peer group. There is no value judgment assigned to performance rankings, other than which category a fund belongs in.

Within that, however, there are ranking grades. Lipper, for example, provides data to many newspapers, including the *Wall Street Journal*, that are based on a fund's total return related to its peers. Any fund in the top 20 percent of its peer group gets an A, the next 20 percent gets a B, and so on.

RATINGS ARE SUBJECTIVE

Ratings involve some type of subjective judgment attached as a kicker to performance. Morningstar, for example, measures performance relative to the risks taken by the fund. It divides the fund universe into four giant groups—U.S. stocks, international stocks, taxable bonds, and municipal bonds—and then awards a five-star rating to the top 10 percent of funds in each group. The next 22.5 percent get four stars, the middle 35 percent get three stars, the next 22.5 percent get two stars, and the lowest 10 percent get one star. A fund must have a three-year track record to get a star rating at all.

> Truth be told, you can generate rankings yourself by going to any number of web sites and searching for funds on the basis of top performance within your search categories.

The firm subsequently assigns a "category rating," which shows how the fund matches up against its most direct competitors. Any number of firms and financial magazines also rate funds using some amalgam of vital statistics. Even the measures of good and bad can be different.

The good news about all of these systems is that they allow for an apples-to-apples comparison of funds. The bad news is that such a comparison is worthless unless you understand what goes into the system. Essentially, each system is looking at past performance, giving the most weight to recent results and then adding some value judgment on top of the numbers. To that end, they look a bit like the performance charts, where what was hot last year will tend to have the highest rating.

A few years ago, for example, about half of all growth-and-income funds tracked by Morningstar long enough to have achieved a star rating carried at least four stars. By comparison, you would have been hard pressed to find a single international fund rated that highly. At that time, a mediocre growth-and-income fund carried four stars but a low category rating, whereas the best international funds had just three stars but got the highest rating for their category.

You also need to understand that Morningstar's system tries to balance risk and reward. I once looked in the firm's performance report and found a bond fund that was near the bottom of its peer group in performance but carried a five-star rating because it took so little risk that its ability to return anything was miraculous. It was a fine fund for anyone looking for the ultimate in safety, but it certainly was not the cream of its peer group.

What's more, none of the ratings services actually claim that its system is predictive. In fact, a Financial Research Corporation study showed there is no real difference in how funds with three-, four-, or five-star ratings from Morningstar perform in the future. The study pointed out that, on average, funds with three stars outperformed five-star issues in 1995, 1996, and 1997. Four-star issues had the best aggregate performance of the group, although even they lost out to funds that were too young to have gained a Morningstar rating.

Another study by Christopher Blake of Fordham University and Matt Morey of Smith College showed that a five-star fund's chances of staying a top performer are no better than a three-star fund's chances of growing into that status; in short, your chances of picking a winner are about the same whether a fund has three, four, or five stars.

"It's not that star ratings are bad," explains James Crandall, a Financial Research analyst, "but they don't predict how a fund will do downstream, and people should not be thinking that a good rating today means great returns in the future."

Whether it's ratings or rankings, one other problem that surfaced with the explosive growth in the number of fund issues is "evaluation devaluation," or the idea that too many funds get top grades. With more than 10,000 mutual funds, too many get high grades. More than ever before, that should make ratings and rankings a jumping-off point rather than a conclusion in the fund-selection process. Instead of just looking for five-star funds, search for those that also have other characteristics you value, such as low expenses and turnover.

In evaluating ratings, see how long the fund has been rated and look for its average score over that time. Funds with a short track record will tend to look better if they have only been around during a boom time like the late 1990s, whereas funds with a long-term track record may suffer from having been open at times when the market was less robust. If the funds look roughly the same, lean toward the one with the longer-term track record, as several studies have shown that funds that show a tendency to top the ratings game over long periods of time may have some enduring edges in performance.

Check, too, to see if the fund has grown dramatically since it first earned a high rating. In short, run the same tests on ratings that you did on past performance and give them about the same weight in the selection process. Anything more puts too much emphasis on how a fund did before you bought it and doesn't pay enough attention to why the fund is right for you going forward.

WRONG-WAY SIGNS

Don't buy a fund expressly because it has a high rating. You should buy the fund because it meets your objectives, expectations, and so on. The rating is a bonus, not a reason to buy.

> *A ranking . . . is like the cover of a book, and perhaps you shouldn't buy books based only on the cover. You'll want to read a review or find someone whose guidance you trust before wasting time and money on the book.*
>
> —MICHAEL LIPPER, FOUNDER OF LIPPER, INC.

17
section

MONEY-MARKET FUNDS

THE EASIEST TYPE OF MUTUAL FUND TO SELECT is the money-market fund. It is the one segment of the fund world where your choice is about greed, not management style and all of the other variables so typical of the normal selection process.

With money funds, you start the analysis with performance and go for the maximum, so long as it comes with the services you need. Pick the best combination of yield and low costs, in a fund that has the check-writing and minimum-balance features you need.

It's that simple.

Here's why:

Money-market mutual funds invest in safe, liquid securities like bank certificates of deposit, government securities, high-grade corporate-financing

> Because you can pick a money fund from the top of the performance charts, finding one is not too hard.

agreements, and other commercial paper that pays money-market interest rates. The fund's net asset value remains a constant $1 per share, and all of the interest comes in the form of new shares plowed into the account.

The rules governing money funds make them virtually all created equal. Some funds generate tax and safety benefits by purchasing only certain assets, such as municipal, government, or insured bonds. Others carry insurance to protect the fund company in the event of a credit crisis.

That protection is important because, unlike bank accounts, money funds are not insured against loss. But generally speaking, money funds are designed to look as much like checking accounts as possible. And while there is no bank insurance, the widely accepted truth in the mutual-fund business is that no significant money fund will ever be allowed to "break the buck," or lose enough money so that its share price falls below $1.

In 1994, during the Orange County bankruptcy, a few funds were poised to break the buck, until their parent companies stepped in. The same thing happened during other threats to credit quality in 1996, 1997, and 1999.

> With virtually no threat for losing principal in money-market funds, the focus turns to returns.

Because all money-market funds operate within the same tightly defined universe, returns don't vary much from one fund to the next. As a result, management distinguishes itself by waiving expenses, sometimes completely.

Let's say the money markets are yielding roughly 6 percent and two funds go out and capture that yield. Both fund companies have expenses of 0.5 percent, about average for money funds, but one company waives half of those expenses. The fund with the waiver can pass 5.75-percent gains to shareholders (the 6-percent money-market yield minus costs), whereas the fund that charges full expenses grows at a rate of 5.50 percent.

It doesn't exactly take a genius to figure out which fund is the better deal. At any given time, half of all money funds are likely to be waiving some or all of their management fees. Those firms want to get investors into the fold and often hope to attract more than just the money-fund dollars.

Strong Funds, for example, frequently has a money fund at or near the top of the return charts, usually on the strength of waived fees. Company executives make no bones about the fact that they want to pitch Strong's other products and services to people drawn in by the prospect of a high-yielding money-market fund.

Waivers don't last forever. Call any fund company that has a high yield and low expenses and ask if the firm is waiving fees and, if so, for how long. You will want to know when fees go up, because that is probably when you will head for the exit.

If you are aiming for extra safety with your investment, you may have to sacrifice some yield and head into a fund invested 100 percent in U.S. Treasuries or insured bonds. And always go with a fund company that you recognize, where you know the pockets are deep. That way, in the unlikely event of some credit problems in the fund, the parent company has the resources to step in and fix the problem without any concern about breaking the buck.

Beyond yield and safety concerns, a money fund is a convenience item, so look for features that match your needs. If you want to have the money ready to move into stocks or other funds, for example, you might pick the fund offered by a fund supermarket or brokerage firm. That way, you have a better chance of moving the money around seamlessly, without having to wait for payment one week and redelivery to a different account days later.

> Most of today's thirty-something investors would rather burn their money than watch it molder in a money-market fund.
> **—James Grant, publisher of Grant's Interest Rate Observer**

If you simply want to use a money fund as a surrogate checking account, examine the transaction and check-writing privileges—from how many you can write in a month to how large they must be to how much it costs if you break the rules. You have to be prepared to meet account minimums, too.

Peter Crane, managing editor at IBC Financial Data in Ashland, Massachusetts, says: "Unlike other funds, this decision is simple: The best yield you can find with the features you want is the fund that gets your money."

STARTING POINTS

Most major and mid-sized newspapers run a list of money-market funds and their current yields once or twice a week. Or check out **www.imoney net.com**, the web site of IBC Financial Data, a service that tracks money-fund rates. At the site, you'll be able to find the top funds, plus their contact numbers.

WRONG-WAY SIGNS

If fees go up, the fund company could be trying to cook you like a frog.

If you want to cook a frog, you don't just throw it in warm water, because it would swim or hop out. Instead, you put it in cool, comforting water and then turn up the heat. By the time the frog realizes there's trouble, it's too late.

Fund companies often cook money-fund investors this way. They lure you in with a fee waiver, then slowly start to add the fees back. Many will hide the extra costs during times of rising interest rates so that your yield stays the same but the extra slice of interest winds up going to the fund firm.

To avoid ending up in hot water with a fund that's no longer a returns leader, be vigilant in reviewing your correspondence from the fund company and watch out for any paperwork that talks of a fee hike. Once the fees get back to the average level—which is about 0.5 percent—it's time to find a new fund with a better deal to offer.

THE LEAST YOU SHOULD REMEMBER

Money funds break the normal selection rules. This is the one time where chasing performance and picking the hot fund is almost always a good idea.

BONDS VERSUS
BOND FUNDS

THE TOUGHEST THING MOST INVESTORS MUST OVERCOME before buying a bond fund is simple: It isn't a stock fund.

Compared to equity funds, bond funds feel stodgy and unglamorous. They are a lower-risk, lower-reward alternative to a stock market that, for the last few years, hasn't exactly felt to most people like it was overloaded with risk.

Bonds, of course, aren't a bad investment, they simply aren't stocks. That made them look bad in the 1990s, but it was a big selling point in the mid-1980s, when bond funds had their heyday.

> With seemingly every stock fund on the rise through the 1990s, bond funds were a tough sell.

Once you get over the but-it's-not-stock hang-up, bonds can be a valuable addition to the portfolio for many investors, providing safety, predictability, and shelter from the ups and downs of the stock market.

Your first decision in bonds comes down to whether you should hold the paper yourself or invest in a fund. The answer depends on a combination of factors, ranging from your knowledge of bonds to how much money you want invested in bonds to the types of bonds you want to buy. Simpler commodity-like bonds are reasonable purchases on your own; raise the bar a bit and start to factor in obscure sectors, small issues, evaluation of credit risk, and other factors, and bond funds will likely carry the day over individual bonds.

To see why that is, let's get down to basics:

Bonds are debt instruments; the issuer borrows your money and promises to pay it back at a set rate over a specified period of time. Safety, regular income, and diversification from the risks of the stock market are bond investing's big selling points.

If you buy individual bonds, you should get the bond's face value if the note is held to maturity. If you need to sell a bond before it matures, however, liquidity could become a problem; the bond market often gives a nasty haircut to investors who bail out. Pricing is almost always tricky, meaning you could pay too much to buy or get less than fair value when selling. And although buying bonds has gotten easier, thanks in large part to the advent of electronic trading at some of the big brokerage houses, it's not necessarily simple or cheap.

By comparison, a bond fund's income stream can change over time, and its share price can swing wildly based on interest-rate activity. The fund never matures, so there is no guaranteed amount to be collected at the end of the rainbow.

But funds offer convenience, the ability to buy in without a lot of money, risk management on many hard-to-figure flavors of bonds, and the chance to reinvest income in a timely fashion rather than having to wait to amass enough to buy a new bond. Amid those pros and cons, it's easy to see why the type of assets should settle your internal bond-versus-fund debate.

> Credit risk is explained in detail in Section 10.

With U.S. Treasury bonds, for example, the only real issue is convenience. Treasuries have no credit risk and Treasury funds practice little professional management. Liquidity is no problem, because Treasury bonds are easily sold. And Treasuries can be purchased directly from the Federal Reserve, usually for much less than the fees you would pay a fund-management company. That's why Treasury bonds generally win out over Treasury funds.

> For information on buying Treasury bonds, bills, and notes yourself. Check out www.treasurydirect.gov.

Likewise, when it comes to insured municipal bonds, a fund's management fees often cost you more than a good manager can earn you back by shopping around. If you are willing to dig and do a lot of research on your own or if you get the help of a financial adviser, corporate bonds become an option as well. And if you want mortgage-backed bonds—bonds made up of mortgage loans—and are willing to stick with Ginnie Maes (slang for GNMA or Government National Mortgage Association bonds), you can probably buy in for a block of $25,000 or more.

The problem with these types of bonds is that they have call features, meaning they face the possibility of being refinanced rather than paid off. When this happens, the value of your bond can change dramatically, or you could get paid off early and have to go shopping for bonds that are, in all likelihood, less attractive yields than what you started with.

Many investors choose to invest in bonds on their own, outside of funds. A 1999 study by the Schwab Center for Investment Research came to the conclusion that bond funds are for people with less than $50,000 in fixed-income investments, who can stomach some volatility in both how much income they get and the value of their principal and who want a fund's mix of convenience and professional management.

> Ultimately, the bonds-versus-funds decision is a matter of choice and personal expertise.

In other words, bond funds are fine until you have enough money to build a diversified portfolio of individual bonds. That said, if you are like most individual investors, you will never have a great grasp of how the junk-bond market works, will never know how to research international bonds, and will never have confidence that you know which mortgage-backed securities are worth owning. You might even run into municipal bonds with complex features and language that affects whether they are good investments.

In those arenas, bond funds are the likely choice, regardless of how much money is at stake. But before buying a bond fund, consider that managers in this arena make little difference and that there is a reason you don't know the name of a "Peter Lynch" mega-star manager who runs a bond fund. In any given year, the difference between the best and worst funds in any bond grouping will be a percentage point or two; in a stock category, the best fund might double your money at the same time the worst fund loses half of it.

Since bond fund performance is less dependent on management, your outcome will be more reliant on expense information. Countless studies have shown a direct correlation between costs and performance, with low-cost bond funds bringing home greater returns. The average bond fund carries a 1.1-percent expense ratio, according to Lipper, Inc.; try to find funds that charge 0.75 percent or less.

Beyond the simple costs, be sure you understand what the fund buys because it may be more than just "bonds." Some bond funds buy "derivative securities," which necessitates further research. (A zero-coupon bond is actually a type of derivative, so don't assume that derivative securities are inherently evil.)

> For detailed information on expenses, see Section 13.

If the fund does not give an open and candid explanation of its derivatives position in its prospectus, call and ask the fund's representatives what these issues are and their upside and downside potential and risk for you, the fund's potential owner. If the fund firm's representatives can't get you an answer that you understand, take a pass on the fund.

According to Mark Riepe, head of the Schwab Center: "If you want fixed-income exposure and know how bonds work, you may be better off on your own. But if you're in the majority of people with no real idea how bonds work, stick with funds."

Driving a car requires a foot on the gas, hands on the wheel and eyes on the road. Navigating the bond market requires a foot on interest rates, a handle on the prospects of being repaid and an eye on inflation.
—STEVEN MINTZ, *The Art of Investing*

TAX EFFICIENCY

MOST PEOPLE THINK THAT THE MOST IMPORTANT ELEMENT of a fund is how much money it makes you. But the really important factor is how much of those gains you actually get to keep.

You may be investing in mutual funds to pay for your retirement or to put your children or grandchildren through college, but the family member who will have the greatest impact on the success of your investment strategy is your Uncle Sam.

> Funds are a "pass-through obligation," meaning that whatever tax liabilities the fund incurs get passed on to you.

A fund incurs tax liabilities when it sells stocks or bonds at a profit or when it receives dividends or interest. That's why a mutual fund's tax efficiency is a key consideration when buying a fund. Unless you hold the fund in a tax-deferred retirement account such as a 401(k) or Individual Retirement Account (IRA), you owe your share of those taxes, even though all you did was hold the fund for the entire year.

> If you sell the fund, you have other potential tax liabilities, which are explained in Section 41.

The end result of the confusing way a fund is taxed is this: If a big chunk of your fund's annual gain is the result of trading stocks—turning over winners to unlock those profits and reinvest them somewhere else—a noticeable piece of your profits will wind up in the pocket of Uncle Sam. How big a piece depends on the way the fund characterizes those gains; anything realized on stocks held more than a year faces a maximum federal tax rate of 20 percent (plus any applicable state taxes). On securities held less than a year, short-term gains are taxed at your ordinary income rate, which is likely to be a lot higher and could run as high as 39.6 percent at the federal level.

> Reinvesting gives you more shares of the fund, which, for tax purposes, acts just as if the fund had cut you a check that you used to pay for those additional shares.

The news is just as bad on your fund's dividends and interest income. They, too, get taxed at your ordinary income rate. And you owe your Uncle Sam even if you reinvested those capital gains and dividends and never touched a penny of the money yourself.

You can even lose money in a fund over the course of a year and yet owe taxes on the "gains" it realized by trading when the market went down. Although the tax laws predate the rules governing mutual funds, it has only been in recent years that investors have fully appreciated how taxes impact their returns. Most fund managers pursue returns without regard to taxes. At the start of 2000, fewer than fifty funds said in their prospectus that they would pursue a tax-efficient investment strategy.

SOME IMPORTANT TAX CONSIDERATIONS

Studies on the effect of taxes vary, although no one disagrees with the idea that paying less in taxes is a good thing whenever possible. That being the case, there are a few tax considerations to make when buying a fund. Examine the following:

1. How much income does the fund generate? Because income is taxed at the highest rate, holding funds that produce a lot of it will result in a big tax

> Past tax efficiency is no guarantee of the future, but it's not a bad indicator.

bill. If you're investing in bonds, look at municipal-bond offerings, which are free from federal taxes. On most stock funds, income is not a big worry, because dividends have become such a small factor in stocks today.

2. What is the fund's capital-gains history?. Some funds consistently minimize taxable gains, pursuing low-turnover strategies and periodically matching the winners they intend to sell with losers that have yet to turn around. However, they may have to deviate from that strategy periodically. Longleaf Partners Fund, for example, has a great long-term record of avoiding Uncle Sam, but it took a big hit in 1999 when it sold stocks that had built up huge long-term gains.

You can also look for funds that put "tax-efficient" or "tax-managed" into their name (and more important, their prospectus). Industry watchers expect that the number of tax-managed funds will skyrocket as more investors come to realize that a 40-percent gain just isn't so grand when you only get to take half of it home.

Lastly, check your fund's web site to see if it posts after-tax return data there. Vanguard introduced this idea late in 1999 and several big fund companies followed suit, showing performance data adjusted for taxes due.

3. What could trigger a tax problem in the fund?   Funds that wind up making big payouts often have one of several common traits. They might, for example, have a new manager, whose housecleaning plans will leave you with a tax hangover. In 1996, for example, Robert Stansky replaced Jeff Vinik as manager of the Fidelity Magellan Fund and made significant changes to the fund's portfolio. The result for the year was an 11.7-percent gain (about half of the Standard & Poor's 500), but a 15.5-percent distribution of assets.

Likewise, whenever a fund announces a strategy shift, a big distribution could be in the offing. When T. Rowe Price Capital Opportunity shifted its focus from mid-cap to large-cap stocks, the resulting sell-off in assets forced the fund to pay out more than 15 percent of its net asset value in distributions.

Shrinking assets and shareholder redemptions can also trigger gains payouts. As investors flee a fund, the manager may be forced to sell stocks in order to meet redemptions. The results can leave remaining shareholders getting bushwhacked by both losses and big capital gains (a nightmare lived by emerging-markets investors in 1998, when the average fund in the category lost 27 percent but still paid out a gains distribution).

Finally, some management strategies make a fund likely to pay big gains in any market conditions. These strategies include flipping stocks quickly, buying heavily into IPOs (that are sold for fast profits), buying mostly merger candidates, or simply managing with a high-turnover style.

> See Section 31 for details on paying taxes on your funds.

4. What are my alternatives?   There are certain types of funds that tend to be inherently tax efficient. Index funds and low-turnover buy-and-hold funds both hold the line on taxable distributions.

Just as important, however, is that you may be able to purchase a tax-inefficient fund in a way that makes taxes a moot point. Consider whether a tax-troublesome fund could go into an IRA, in one of its many forms, at which point the gains are sheltered and the fund's tax efficiency becomes a nonissue.

5. What time of year is it?   Once you get to the fall, a fund will have put up a lot of the numbers it can expect for the year, particularly when it comes to gains distributions. If you buy a fund late in the year but before it passes out gains to shareholders, your big welcome to the fund could be in the form of taxes due. That's right, if you buy the fund the day before the distribution, you share in the taxes as if you had owned the fund for the entire year.

> Any time you look to buy a fund late in the year, examine whether you should put off the purchase until after distributions are made.

To avoid any such unpleasant surprises, call the fund companies and ask if they anticipate paying out taxable gains this year. If so, get an estimate on how much (most firms make guesses at their gains payout late in the year) and when the gain will be paid. Some fund firms also post these numbers on their web sites.

Funds generally make their payouts in November and December. If the estimated gain is small, there may be no reason to put off buying the fund. If it's large, you may want to wait or consider another, more tax-efficient fund altogether.

6. Do I care about this fund's tax efficiency?   Saving money on taxes is great, but not if it comes at the expense of making money. If you think a fund's returns are potentially strong enough so that you can absorb the tax bill and still come out on top of other funds, you've sold yourself and shouldn't let taxes come in the way.

Just as some funds overcome high expenses to deliver great returns, so other funds overcome tax burdens.

THE LEAST YOU SHOULD REMEMBER

You will owe taxes due based on what the fund does. On average, that can eat away 1 to 2 percentage points of your total return, but in a worst-case scenario, it will eat away your entire profit in the fund over a year or you will owe taxes on a fund that actually lost money.

THE RIGHT WAY TO PROCEED

Examine a fund's history of paying out gains, its turnover, and its investment strategy. If those three things point to a fund that will leave you owing a lot of your profit to Uncle Sam, either stick the fund in a tax-deferred account or look for a competitor that scores better on the high-tax warning signs.

> *You have to look at these [tax-managed] funds on the basis of what you earn after taxes, but it's a moot point if they can't generate good returns before taxes.*

— DON PHILLIPS, PRESIDENT OF MORNINGSTAR, INC.

section

RETIREMENT ACCOUNTS

I T'S EASIER TO SAY WHAT TO KEEP OUT of your retirement accounts than to tell you what to put in them. What goes into a retirement account, after all, depends on personal factors like risk tolerance, time until retirement, and so on. What's more, you may be limited by the options available in your retirement plan, with some 401(k) and other types of retirement programs offering as few as three investment options.

But because the big idea behind retirement savings is the tax advantage of growing your money in a tax-deferred (or in the case of a Roth IRA, tax-free) environment, it's easy to see what kinds of funds to eliminate or scale back on in your retirement savings.

It's a little more difficult to see what belongs in your retirement plan, because you can raise a question about even the most conventional and seemingly obvious selections.

That said, let's look at the broad types of funds—those that don't belong in your retirement portfolio, those that may have a place, and those that probably should play a role.

OBVIOUS NO-NO'S FOR YOUR RETIREMENT ACCOUNTS

Tax-Free Bond Funds

There's a reason why tax-frees aren't usually an option in 401(k) and other retirement programs, but it's surprising how often this mistake is made in IRAs by people who aren't quite clear about the rules.

The big plus for tax-advantaged retirement accounts is that your money grows without the diluting effect of taxes. Tax-exempt funds have that feature built in. But redundancy is just the start. In a tax-free fund, you are trading a lower yield for the improved tax situation. Because you don't need the fund's tax protection in an IRA or 401(k), however, that lower payback means you are sacrificing earnings power for nothing.

> If tax-free bond funds appeal to you, use them outside of an IRA, where you can really reap their benefits.

Worse yet, you pay taxes on income when you withdraw it from a retirement account, which means that your low tax-free income actually becomes taxable.

That's ugly. Just as you don't carry two umbrellas in the rain, there is no need to have tax-advantaged funds in accounts that are structured to give you tax advantages.

Guaranteed Investment Contracts (GICs)

Sometimes known as stable-value accounts or guaranteed-interest accounts, about the only guarantee they really provide is that your money's buying power will be swallowed by inflation over the years. In retirement accounts, the idea is to tie your money up for years and let it grow and work. As a result, keeping the money in cash—which is really what a GIC is doing—is self-defeating, making it hard for you to grow the money to the point where it can provide a suitable nest egg.

Regardless, these are offered in roughly two-thirds of all 401(k)-like retirement programs and account for roughly half of the dollars invested in those plans. Furthermore, many of these assets are in the accounts for the wrong reason, meaning that the investor believes that their principal is "guaranteed," much like a bank certificate of deposit.

The guarantee applies to the interest rate returned on the investment, not to the principal; a default is highly unlikely, so people buying these investments for safety's sake are not necessarily getting what they pay for.

Money-Market Funds

Money funds are an inappropriate choice for a retirement account for all of the same reasons that GICs are a poor choice. Essentially, a money-market fund is an investment in cash when retirement assets should be invested in securities with a chance for more long-term growth.

NOT-SO-OBVIOUS NO-NO'S FOR YOUR RETIREMENT ACCOUNTS

Company Stock Funds

The biggest chunk of money in 401(k) plans is held in the employer's stock, roughly one-fourth of all retirement-plan dollars. (That's a bit more than is invested in guaranteed investment contracts or diversified stock funds.)

The problem with company stock is not that it's a poor investment, because it can be a terrific choice depending on your employer. And in some cases, workers have no choice but to invest in company stock, since that is the way their employer matches the contributions of employees. But in terms of volatility, the company stock fund is an eggs-in-one-basket approach to investing. That effect is concentrated further because your employer's fortunes determine both your current income (salary) and future income.

"You may get great performance in the company stock, but you also have the most volatility and risk there," says David L. Wray, president of the Chicago-based Profit Sharing/401(k) Council of America. "If you invest heavily there, you must be especially vigilant and ready to change—and you have to make sure your feelings for the company don't cloud your decisions."

> Significant investment in company stock funds is not appropriate for your retirement portfolio because if the company has a setback, it could jeopardize both your job and your investment.

If your company has an employee stock-ownership plan—many of which allow you to buy shares at a discount, outside of the retirement plan—that usually will be the best way for you to take stock in your employer. Otherwise, limit your holdings in company stock to no more than 15 percent of your retirement portfolio, which is enough to participate in the company's success without doing too much damage to your future if the company ever gets into trouble.

Low-Turnover, Low-Yield Growth Funds

We've spent much of this book praising funds that have low-turnover and don't produce much income. However, those funds are best for taxable accounts, where a buy-and-hold strategy allows stocks to appreciate without generating much in the way of current tax obligations.

> Your retirement savings should be your investments with the longest time horizon. This is where you can afford to take the most risk, so allow yourself to be aggressive.

Because the taxable output is small, the benefits of holding these funds in your retirement plans is muted. By comparison, you get the maximum tax advantage by sheltering your shoot-for-the-moon, high-turnover funds.

If you own both types of funds, put the least tax-efficient funds into your retirement accounts; funds that are not tax-efficient gain that efficiency when held in a retirement account.

OBVIOUS CHOICES FOR YOUR RETIREMENT ACCOUNTS AND THE NOT-SO-OBVIOUS QUESTIONS ABOUT THEM

Bond Funds

There is a lot of disagreement as to whether bond funds belong in retirement accounts at all, and you will find plenty of experts who say they don't. But a growing number are equally convincing that bond funds are an appropriate choice, particularly as your time horizon shortens and you have less time to ride out the vagaries of the stock market before you will have to pull the money from your retirement accounts.

Unlike stock funds, bond funds get most of their returns from income, which is taxed at ordinary income tax rates (up to 39.6 percent at the federal level). Sheltering that income allows the money in the account to grow without the drag of taxes, which is a plus.

Nonetheless, don't turn to bond funds thinking they are the "safe" choice. Not only are bond funds potentially volatile, but they typically produce a lower long-term return than stock funds. That's a big risk-reward trade-off, and one that's not worth making with too much of your retirement portfolio.

In other words, bond funds really should become a serious option only as you near retirement age, say within ten years of taking distributions.

Stock Funds, Particularly Aggressive Ones

This is the obvious choice, the standard advice, and it is usually right.

As just noted, however, the reality depends on your time horizon. Stock funds get most of their returns from capital appreciation, and those long-term capital gains are taxed at 20 percent when they occur outside of a retirement plan.

Inside a retirement account—with the exception of a Roth IRA, where the money is not taxed when it is withdrawn—those gains are taxed as income when they are distributed. That means that an investor actually could wind up paying a higher tax rate on these funds than if they were held in a taxable account. Logically, you might conclude that this situation makes bond funds the most attractive choice for your retirement money, but a 1999 T. Rowe Price study showed just the opposite.

"Essentially, the disadvantage of subjecting the stock funds' earnings to higher ordinary income tax rates at retirement is offset by the advantage of deferring taxes for many years on their higher compounded earnings growth," the study says. In plain English, however, that means that the best choice for assets will depend on both tax bracket and time horizon. The lower your tax bracket in retirement and the longer your investing period, the more likely it is that a stock fund is your best choice.

Index Funds

At first blush, this seems contradictory, given that a few minutes ago we questioned the value of low-turnover, low-yield funds in the retirement portfolio. That criticism aside, index funds are the autopilot of the retirement plan, the way to get yourself stock-market returns in an easy, straightforward fashion.

In addition, these funds have the big advantage of low costs, which adds up over the long years you will salt this money away in your retirement account.

> If you are faced with limited choices in a retirement plan and aren't too happy with your options, leaning heavily on the index funds in the mix is almost always the way to go.

Funds You Take a Flyer On

Almost anything can fit into this category, from a high-risk sector fund to a market-timing fund to international or regional offerings. They may not be available in your employer-sponsored retirement plan, but they are perfect for a retirement account.

The reasons for this aren't much different than those for a basic aggressive-growth fund, except that you are more likely to turn over funds that fall into this category. When the hot sector falls on hard times, you are likely to dump the fund to move on, and that would trigger a taxable event, were it not for their being in a retirement account.

By putting these types of funds into your retirement plan, you can fool around with your "fun money" and not take a beating on taxes.

SOMETHING TO CONSIDER

When it comes to your time horizon, keep in mind that you're retiring, not dying. Don't invest as if the day you hit retirement age is the day you no longer need the money. If you're lucky, you have a few decades of time horizon left; your retirement accounts will remain a good place for your most aggressive money throughout that time span.

WRONG-WAY SIGNS

If more than half of your tax-deferred retirement savings—plans at work and IRAs—is in GICs, money-market accounts, and bond funds, you are in serious danger of having your purchasing power shrink to the point where you could outlive your money. Your retirement savings should be your investments with the longest time horizon. This is where you can afford to take the most risk, so allow yourself to be aggressive.

THE RIGHT WAY TO PROCEED

Build a diversified retirement portfolio by investing first in stock funds, including large- and small-stock funds, domestic and international holdings. Be as aggressive as you can while letting yourself sleep at night. As you age and your time horizon to retirement shrinks to ten years or less, begin to add a bond component to your holdings. Spice up the whole thing with some company stock, if offered, but leave the tax-free and "guaranteed" investments to someone else.

> *One thousand dollars left to earn interest at 8 percent a year will grow to $43 quadrillion in 400 years, but the first hundred years are the hardest.*
>
> —SIDNEY HOMER, LATE FOUNDER OF
> THE BOND RESEARCH DEPARTMENT AT SALOMON BROTHERS

21

section

RISK MEASURES

YOU HAVE LEARNED TO SIZE UP A FUNDS based on costs, past performance, ratings and rankings, and how they meet your objectives and fit into a portfolio. One last test before buying is to evaluate your potential purchase based on what the academic community calls "measures of risk."

Truth be told, finding these measures is easy. They are usually available from the fund company itself or from a ratings service like Morningstar. The hard part is understanding what the heck you're looking at.

Here's what they are all about:

Measuring Risk

For most people looking at some type of risk measurement, there are four different elements to consider: standard deviation, R-squared, beta, and alpha.

Standard deviation. Standard deviation shows how far, based on its history, a fund is likely to vary from its average return. Think of a bell curve, where the peak is the average performance and there are an equal number of return periods on either side of the average. Statistically speaking, we can expect the fund's performance to fall within two standard deviations from the mean roughly 95 percent of the time.

What does that actually mean?

For simplicity's sake, let's examine an imaginary fund that winds up with returns in round numbers. The first year, it gains nothing. The next year it gains

10 percent, and the third year it gains 20 percent. The average return over this period is 10 percent. That is therefore the standard deviation.

Now let's go back to the statement "We can expect the fund's performance to fall within two standard deviations from the mean roughly 95 percent of the time." Two standard deviations on our imaginary fund would be 20 percent in either direction. So, if you were shopping for this fund and examined its standard deviation, you would come to the conclusion that your worst loss is likely to be no more than 10 percent (the 10-percent average minus two times the standard deviation of 10), whereas your biggest gain is not likely to be more than 30 percent (the average gain plus two standard deviations).

> As with anything else that uses past performance to set its scale, standard deviation can swing wildly, depending on how many time periods are considered and how well the fund did during the years considered.

The bigger the standard deviation, the wider the likely performance swings from its average past performance. When it comes to funds, standard deviation is generally calculated for monthly returns over a specific time period—usually thirty-six months—with the results then modified to produce an annualized result.

R-squared.   This is an academic term that refers to the portion of the fund's return that can be explained away by the movement of an index.

Without delving too deeply into investment math, consider that the Vanguard 500 Index has an R-squared of 100 when compared to the Standard & Poor's 500 Index. This is hardly surprising, since the fund is modeled to mimic the index. What that perfect match means is that whenever the index has gone up, so has the fund.

If the fund has an R-squared of less than 80 compared to an index, it means the fund and the index don't behave that much alike, although it could also mean that the fund is being compared against the wrong benchmark. The average gold fund, for example, has an R-squared of 3 against the Standard & Poor's Index, which makes sense because gold funds could not attribute much of their performance to the S&P.

Beta.   Even when compared to the correct index, what R-squared does not show is the degree of movement against the index. That's where beta comes

in. Beta gives you insight into how risky a fund can be relative to the benchmark.

The benchmark is considered to have a beta of 1.0, so a fund with a beta of
1.0 would be expected to track the movement of the
index exactly. If the market went up 10 percent, therefore, you would expect the fund do to the same. By
comparison, a fund with a beta of 1.5 percent is much
more volatile than the market. When the market rises
or falls 10 percent, this kind of high-beta fund would
be expected to move 15 percent (in whatever direction

> Beta measures risk or
> volatility of a fund
> relative to the market.

the market goes). Conversely, a fund with a beta of 0.5 would be expected to
gain 5 percent when the market grows by 10 percent, but it would lose just 5
percent when the market takes a 10 percent correction.

Beta is not an indicator of good or bad. Also, it is only meaningful if the R-
squared is high. If the fund does not achieve most of its movements in concert
with an index, its beta compared to that index is worthless (because it really
isn't expected to move when that index moves).

Alpha. Without getting bogged down in the esoteric minutia of this calculation, here's what you
need to know: A positive alpha *implies* that the
manager did better than might have been expected,
given the risks taken, whereas a negative alpha *suggests* that the manager could have done better, considering the risks investors were exposed to.

> Alpha is a statistical effort
> to measure whether the
> manager has added any
> value by delivering more
> returns than you might
> expect, given the fund's
> level of risk.

Having been exposed to all of this academic
brain-twisting, the big question is how to use the
information. Here are some things to consider:

- When looking at a fund's beta, examine the returns of the index to get
  an idea of what kind of performance you can expect. Look at the index's best and worst years, then multiply those returns by the beta to
  get an idea of what you might expect the range of returns to be. If you
  want to take this test further, compare this number to the fund's standard deviation. The risk measures should combine to give you a good
  means of framing possible returns.

- Funds with a low R-squared can often bring diversification to your portfolio. Thus, if you have funds that are heavy in large-company stocks and that have close ties to the S&P 500, you might look for funds with a low R-squared.
- If a fund has an R-squared of 100 and a beta of roughly 1.0, chances are that you will be better off in an index fund. The index offering is most likely to have lower costs and greater efficiency for the same predicted returns.

THE LEAST YOU SHOULD REMEMBER

None of these risk tools actually determine whether a fund is good or bad for you to own. About the only general conclusion you can draw is that high standard deviations and betas generally indicate more volatile funds and that anyone who fears volatility might prefer to stay away from such funds.

Before swearing off high-beta funds, keep in mind that volatility works in both directions. Investors will groan when a fund endures a 10-percent stock-market correction but will feel redeemed when their fund is going up at a 15-percent-plus annual clip with the market.

SOMETHING TO CONSIDER

Plenty of investors—including financial advisers—ignore these risk measures altogether and assemble efficient investment portfolios. What you get out of using these numbers should be a sense of security that you are picking a fund that can meet your expectations. If this academic approach simply serves to make you nervous, you might be better off ignoring it altogether.

REGISTERING YOUR FUND PURCHASE

OF ALL THE CHOICES YOU MUST MAKE when choosing a fund, the last place you would expect to make an error is in the way you put your name on the paperwork. Yet this simple step—one that transforms you from potential buyer to owner—could leave you open to future problems based on how you register your investment.

Registering your account is an estate-planning is-sue. The idea is to maximize what goes to your heirs and avoid the headaches of probate. Although laws vary by state, mutual-fund holdings typically are sub-ject to probate. By law, you can pass an unlimited amount of assets to a spouse, free of estate taxes. The amount you can pass to nonspouses will reach $1 million come 2006.

> Probate is the state judicial process that determines the value of a deceased's estate.

So, say a couple has $1.5 million in assets, all registered jointly. The husband dies, the wife inherits everything, and there is no tax. But when the wife dies, at least $500,000 (more if this happens before 2006) will be hit with taxes of 40-plus percent.

If the couple had created "bypass trusts," the assets could have been split, each partner having a trust for their half. When the husband dies, the trust holds the money, with income given to the wife. When she dies,

> Much more on tax issues in Sections 31 and 41.

the principal is distributed—without estate taxes—according to instructions laid out when the trust was created. Her assets, also below the taxable limit, get passed on without estate taxes, too, thereby writing Uncle Sam out of the will.

> Consult an accountant or estate-planning attorney about the right type of registration for your situation and your state.

The bottom line is that you should not register assets emotionally but instead should get help to determine the best course of action for your heirs. In addition, you need to realize that many funds don't list all registration options on their paperwork, meaning you must find out whether you need additional forms or whether you can submit a letter to get the account registered the way you want.

Lastly, state laws affect registration. Community-property states, for example, have their own rules. And many states don't allow all types of ownership, meaning that registering your fund for, say, "transfer on death," might not be enough to protect your assets.

REGISTRATION OPTIONS

To get you started, here are the registration options you are likely to find on most fund account applications:

Sole ownership.   This is a self-explanatory term. All responsibilities rest with the individual. When the owner dies, assets are distributed in accordance with his or her will (or divided according to state succession laws if the owner dies without a will).

Joint tenants with rights of survivorship.   This is how most couples register shares. This lets one or more people—related or not—share ownership; when one dies, the shares avoid probate and pass directly to the survivor (although the amount still counts toward the value of the estate). If you change registration from sole to joint with anyone other than your spouse, you have made a gift. If more than $10,000 is involved, that has tax consequences.

Tenants in common.   These partners share ownership, but by a specified amount (not necessarily a 50-50 split). When one partner dies, the money goes to the estate, not the survivor, and is passed along according to instructions in the will.

Tenancy by the entirety.   This arrangement is similar to joint tenancy but is more common in real estate, where legal nuances make it preferable. The property passes directly to a surviving spouse, without probate. It is available only to married couples.

Residents in states with community-property laws can register accounts as such. When one spouse dies, his or her portion is divided equally between the survivor and the estate. All of that money is valued at the date of death, however, meaning the survivor can redeem some of the couple's joint holdings without facing the full tax brunt of accrued capital gains.

In community-property states, dealing with taxes can be tricky no matter how your shares are registered. Moreover, if you set up accounts as community property and move to a state where it is not the law, you almost certainly will have to reregister everything to avoid a potential estate nightmare.

Transfer on death.   This is also self-explanatory. The shares go to a named beneficiary without probate, although the money counts toward the value of the estate.

Gift-to-Minors Account.   To establish an account for a minor child without going through the complications of setting up a trust, register in the name of the child and a custodian (not necessarily the parents) under either the Uniform Transfer to Minors Act (UTMA) or Uniform Gift to Minors Act (UGMA). As applied to funds, there is little difference between the acts—in some states, UTMA supplements UGMA; in others it supplants UGMA—except that the date when the minor takes control of the account may vary from eighteen to twenty-one, depending on the state you live in.

The money belongs to the child the instant it is given, although the custodian remains in control of the account until the child becomes an adult.

Trust accounts.   These arrangements require establishment of a formal trust. Most fund families require legal documentation that the trust exists. If you establish a trust, you will have to reregister existing assets for the trust to be considered part of the agreement. Making this change in registration is easy. Call the fund group and ask for the forms or send a letter of instructions with a signature guarantee. The move is not taxable (unless it's a large gift to a nonspouse). Failure to reregister however, can be costly; the best estate plans are shot to pieces if holdings are not retitled into the trusts.

A MISTAKE TO AVOID

If you have gone to the trouble of establishing trusts, your funds need to be registered into those trusts or they don't get the shelter you were seeking for them.

Many people pay for the estate planning but wind up leaving the trusts vacant by not retitling their assets. If you have a trust and aren't sure if your assets have been registered properly, look at your statements. It should describe how the account is registered—possibly with an acronym like JTWROS for joint tenancy—right where it shows your name.

SOMETHING TO CONSIDER

Not only will you want to register the fund properly, but you will want to register yourself for the fund services that are important to you. Most funds offer telephone redemption and switching privileges, for example, but they may require that you check off the option on your account application.

If you don't do it when you open the account, you'll have to take care of it in writing at a later date, and most people only find out that they have a problem at the very time they need to make a move. To avoid those problems, consider all of the options the fund offers, especially those covering the ways for you to exit the fund when the time comes.

PART TWO

WHEN YOU OWN

KEEPING A FILE ON
YOUR FUNDS

MOST FUND OWNERS MAKE A COMMON MISTAKE within minutes of mailing their account paperwork. Once they have written the check and sealed the envelope, they think the work is over. It's not. There's one more key piece of the puzzle to complete—creating and maintaining a working file for the fund.

It's a simple matter but is often overlooked. The first thing that should go in your files is a detailed list of the reasons you bought the fund and the expectations you had for it at the time of purchase.

When reviewing your eventual satisfaction with a fund, you will need to answer the question "Would I buy the fund again today?" That's tough to answer as the years pass and the precise factors in your decision get a little fuzzy.

For example, you might have picked a fund for its Morningstar rating, its track record, and its asset class, but you also might have chosen it because it had a low minimum initial investment and because you needed to diversify more. Ten years from now, however, you may have amassed enough money not to care about low minimums, the Morningstar ratings may have changed, and your portfolio might have diversified as it has grown.

As your reasons for buying fade over time, the sole focus tends to become performance, which means your future decisions will be based almost entirely on current numbers. That's why when many investors hit a patch of bad performance in an otherwise good fund, they ask themselves the pained question "What was I thinking" and end up making a poor sell decision because they can't actually remember the thought process that led to the purchase in the first place.

STARTING YOUR FILE

With that in mind, start your file by writing down the reasons you bought it. To effectively review your fund selections later, answer these questions in writing:

How did I hear about the fund? If performance is disappointing, you will want to consider whether you still have confidence in the initial referral. Your investment newsletter might have dumped the fund, or Morningstar might have downgraded it.

> If you buy a fund for a specific reason, you should sell it only if it is not delivering what you expected or if you no longer need what it provides.

What specific performance traits made me want the fund? Buying a fund that sits atop the one-year performance charts is different from buying one that has consistently finished in the top 20 percent of its peer group. You should record ratings from a service like Morningstar or Value Line, which measure risk-adjusted performance.

Be as clear as possible about the performance traits that made you want this fund; if the fund loses that status, then it has lost some of the luster that first attracted you.

What are my expectations and benchmarks for this fund? You might want to beat the market or to beat nine of ten funds in the same asset class. Or you might want a simple 8-percent annual return. Either way, you want a fund that meets your goals, so lay out those expectations in terms of both absolute returns and performance against peers or benchmarks.

In the market boom of the late 1990s, I was amazed by the number of people who claimed to have bought a fund hoping for a 10-percent return but who dumped the fund after 15-percent gains simply because it had not done as well as some of its peers. Laying out expectations helps you tune out the market noise.

What should a bad year look like?   Predict the worst-case shortfall in a market downturn. (Short cut: Put a minus sign in front of the return during the fund's best-ever gain. This helps you decide whether a fund is too volatile or risky for you; later on, it tells you whether a slump is a big disappointment or within the realm of your expectations.

What characteristics make it attractive to me?   Low minimums, no sales or marketing fees, or availability through a specific funds supermarket can influence your thinking. So can low expense and turnover ratios and other cost factors. Over time, however, funds change policies and you have changing needs. If the characteristics that once drew you to a fund are no longer important or if the fund changes key traits (by raising costs or increasing turnover), it becomes easy to justify a move to a better-performing competitor.

> A fund that consistently meets your expectations is probably worth holding, even if it lags the market or no longer sits at the very top of the performance charts.

What role is this fund supposed to play in my portfolio?   This is the specific role you had picked for a fund, its job within your portfolio.

Assume you bought a fund to diversify. As the years pass and you buy other funds, you may have overlap and the fund may no longer serve its original function. Another possibility is that the fund itself will move from one type of asset to another, buying large-company stocks today when it invested in small stocks when you first bought it. In this case, you need to re-assess the place of this fund in your portfolio.

> If the fund no longer serves the purpose for which you bought it, you may not want to own it anymore.

Are there any other attractions to this fund?   Note whether the manager is a star, whether the fund buys a hot type of asset, or whether there are any other significant selection factors. Over time, the manager may leave and the assets may fall out of favor. In all cases, you will want to be able to answer the "What was I thinking?" question with some level of certainty so that you can make sensible choices as an owner.

BUILDING YOUR FILE

After starting your mutual-fund file by writing down the reasons you first invested, you'll use the file to store items such as:

> If you keep no file on your funds or your records are missing the very basics, call your fund company and ask for duplicates.

A copy of the account application. This should show you precisely how the account was registered and the features you signed up for. Staple a copy of the account application to the prospectus that came with it so that you have a good idea of what you were looking at—including the cost structure—when you opened the account.

The most recent prospectus or proxy statement. On the off chance that anything unexpected happens with the fund in the short term, you will want more than the superficial numbers on your account statements. The most recent prospectus and proxy statements will quickly show you what the fund manager says about performance and prospects, as well as any changes that have taken place over time. Ultimately, the most recent prospectus may best be viewed by comparing it to the first one you got from the company.

Applicable tax documents. If you own the fund as part of an IRA account, you will get confirmations of the amount of your annual deposit. Your tax preparer will thank you for keeping those documents once the time comes to move money around or make withdrawals. Tax documents also include any letters of instruction that you write when selling a partial stake in the fund using the "specific selection" method.

Your year-end account statement, plus all monthly or quarterly statements for the current year. The year-end statement is a de facto tax document because it shows all activity in the fund during the year, including purchases, redemptions, dividends, and capital gains, as well as the dates of any transactions.

A good file will have the monthly or quarterly statements from the current year only. When the year-end statement arrives, the sheets that the fund has sent in the preceding eleven months get thrown out; over time, you will have only the final statement from each year, which will provide you with a concise and accurate history of your activity in the fund.

Trading confirmations or check stubs from any partial withdrawals.   Long term, this information most likely will not be necessary, but in the short term, it's a good safeguard against trouble. If you make a trade by telephone or over the Internet, keep a copy of any and all documentation showing the timing of the transaction, the shares involved, and the confirmation order for your number.

> Once you have the year-end document, there is no reason to keep the monthly or quarterly statements, as they show only partial results and will not be useful in the long term.

If a trade is not processed properly, having this detail—plus having included the name of the phone rep you talk to if you transact business by phone—will speed up the process of getting the problem fixed.

Armed with all of these data in your file on a fund, there is very little that you can face as an owner that you will not be prepared to deal with.

THE RIGHT WAY TO PROCEED

If you don't have a list of the reasons you bought the funds in your portfolio, try to reconstruct such a list now. The exercise is likely to prove how hard it is to remember a lot of the specific details that drove your thinking.

If you don't have a file containing your account history, make one. The sooner you reconstruct your records, the easier it will be. If you wait until you need the information to recover the missing data, it could be more difficult and costly.

MONITORING YOUR FUNDS

THE MOST IMPORTANT THING YOU CAN DO with your funds once you've selected them is to leave them alone. If you watch them every day, you lose perspective and start to see daily events as having long-term significance. That leads you to be more likely to make an unnecessary move, which is why so many studies show that investors tend to buy a fund after it has already posted a sharp increase and sell immediately after a downturn.

Furthermore, daily data usually arrive without context. Your fund may take a nosedive during a market downturn, but that decline may be less than the average fund in its asset class. When you studied the fund as a buyer, you looked at the last year, three years, five years, and ten years of gains. Nowhere did you study what the fund did on an average daily basis.

> A mere market decline does not signal trouble; you knew that downturns were possible when you bought the fund, and a lifetime investor expects to live through several investment cycles.

With that in mind, watching your mutual funds should become an exercise that is centered around watching for warning signs instead of monitoring short-term price appreciation.

Michael Stolper of Stolper Asset Management in San Diego notes that most investors should act as though they are going into a coma. "Pick a fund that you can live without touching for twenty years. When you come out of your coma after that long, if you picked the right fund to begin with, you're going to be very happy."

Since you aren't going to be comatose while you own the fund, the best thing you can do is develop a series of things to look for that help you determine whether the fund you picked is failing to do its job. Absent these warning signs, the fund is probably doing what you bought it to do.

Here are the elements that should put a fund onto your "watch list," a designation that signals that it needs to be examined more closely because something appears amiss. Going onto the watch list does not make a fund worth dumping; it's simply a "yellow-alert" status on a defensive scale where increased danger spurs the "red alert" of a sale.

WATCH-LIST CANDIDATES

Put a fund on your watch list whenever:

Performance starts to lag.   Everything that affects a fund eventually hits the bottom line, so lackluster returns light the caution sign.

Compare a fund to both its peers and its own history. Volatility is a way of life for some funds; if yours has a history of good returns with occasional lapses, it is less worrisome than when a steady winner falls behind.

> Experts disagree about how long to stick with an ailing fund. Give a proven performer at least six months—and up to two years—to regain its touch.

Most people factor Morningstar's star ratings into their buying equation. The key Morningstar tool for relative performance is the "category rating," which measures a fund against its competition; if the whole asset class is faltering and your fund doesn't smell as bad as its peers, that's actually a reason to hold on. Without the comparison to peers, you don't have enough context to make a decision based on short-term numbers.

Obviously, you can stop worrying about performance if the fund rebounds. If returns don't improve and the fund lags its peers, moving on becomes a real consideration.

The manager leaves.   You shouldn't sell a fund just because the manager has left, but you need to watch the fund more closely whenever there is a move in this key position.

Unless the fund has been a laggard (in which case you *want* a shake-up), you are looking to see whether the new manager will steer the ship with a steady hand or change the fund's course.

G. Edward Noonan of Triad Investment Advisory in Hingham, Massachusetts, says: "Watch performance, looking for an evolution in how the fund operates. Once you know the change hasn't damaged the fund, take it off your [watch] list."

The fund company gets taken over.   This has less direct impact than losing your fund manager, but new top brass sometimes changes how a fund is run, tying a manager's hands or changing the available research pipeline. Also, takeovers can spur manager departures. If the old manager can't work in the new environment, you may not want to invest there, either. Furthermore, if the new owner has a similar fund, you are likely to see the two merged. That's not necessarily bad news for investors, but it bears watching because you may wind up in a fund with different rules and a slightly different take on the market than the one you picked in the first place.

> If a fund is getting big, watch its portfolio carefully to see whether it continues to do the job you bought it for.

Assets surge.   Bigger funds buy bigger stocks. That's a problem if you want a fund that buys small- or mid-sized stocks. Any time a small-company fund crosses the $1-billion mark, it is likely to drift toward medium-sized companies. When mid-cap funds hit $2 billion to $5 billion, they drift toward giant stocks. The fund may continue to be a good performer, but if it no longer fits into your plans or if it gives you overlap in one asset class and a vacuum in another, then it's not the fund you need.

The fund closes to new investors.   Fund closures are supposed to protect investors by keeping a fund true to its investment objective. But they sometimes happen too late, after the fund has passed its optimum size. In that case, cutting off new investors won't make the fund small and nimble again.

In addition, the lack of new cash sometimes inhibits a manager, forcing the sale of securities to meet redemptions.

As Thurman Smith of Equity Fund Research in Malden, Massachusetts, puts it: "If a fund closes and you see deterioration in performance, you have a partial explanation that makes it easier to say good-bye."

The fund reopens.   This would seem to contradict the last condition, but it doesn't. If the fund closed for the right reason—to protect the interests of shareholders—then find out why it's reopening.

Whenever a fund does something out of character—say, hiking expense ratios or marketing fees or doubling its turnover rate—proceed with caution.

If this is an anomalous event, drop the yellow flag within a year. But if this warning sign is coupled with other signals—most notably, poor performance—you have a problem.

You receive a proxy statement seeking to change the fund.   Funds need your permission by proxy to change their objective or the types of securities they buy. A proxy vote automatically fires up the warning lamp. In most cases, the changes are nothing to be concerned about, but if an underperforming fund is asking for more leeway to invest in new areas, it's a sign that the manager is feeling boxed in and might be searching for a way to break the traditional discipline of the fund.

If a proxy is passed and the fund starts to change its holdings, you can draw the conclusion that the manager is looking for a way out of the strategy that drew you into the fund in the first place. If the manager wants out, you may want out, too.

> Section 34 discusses the rules of proxy statements.

Your objectives change.   Much of your satisfaction with a fund is derived from specific needs and comfort levels. The same fund that has been appropriate for you during the last ten years may not be a good fit in the future.

If your focal point is changing, watch your funds less from a performance standpoint than from the standard of your new agenda. The fund may still be just fine—but no longer appropriate for you. If this impression grows over time, it's a clear signal that the fund will not make it off your watch list.

But don't be too quick to dump your funds based on short-term market moves. There is no guarantee that your next fund will be any better than the one you are thinking of selling, because it's being picked by the same person whose last selection didn't work out too well.

THE RIGHT WAY TO PROCEED

Do a complete portfolio review once or twice a year, preferably when the fund sends you a new prospectus. Having the most current paperwork allows you to gauge factors beyond performance and to hear management's explanation for recent performance.

WRONG-WAY SIGNS

If you are turning over your fund portfolio with any frequency (selling more than one fund in any year), you are either picking funds badly or overmanaging the ones you have. If you picked the funds using a sound methodology, you should not interfere with their ability to deliver according to your expectations.

ASSET ALLOCATION

MANY INVESTORS TRY TO BUILD A PORTFOLIO OF FUNDS by following the sample asset allocation they see in a newsletter or magazine or by using a rule of thumb. They are playing financial Jeopardy, looking for answers before they have asked the right questions. If you start the process by asking, say, "How much should I put into aggressive-growth funds?" you almost certainly will get an answer that looks good in someone's formula but has little bearing on your ability to reach your goals.

Instead, think of asset allocation as financial alchemy. It brings together your money, your needs, your hopes, and your risk tolerances.

> Asset allocation may be the most critical decision you make regarding your fund portfolio—how you spread your money around has more to do with your returns than the actual funds you pick to do the job.

While asset allocation does not fit all, one methodology for determining a good allocation probably does. It's a discovery process that has more to do with you than with the funds you own or are considering for the future.

Ask yourself the following five questions:

1. What do I want to happen in my financial future?
2. When do I want it to happen?
3. What does it cost?
4. How much money do I have now?
5. How much money can I expect to have when the time comes?

Ultimately, asset allocation boils down to what it is going to take to go from where you are now to where you want to be in the future. By developing an allocation, you set a course to reach your goals.

> When it comes to retirement planning, always invest as if you will live to be at least 100, which gives you a reasonable chance of not outliving your money.

So, let's say you are thirty-five years old today with $250,000 in investable assets and you look into the future and determine that you will need $2 million at age sixty-five in order to live out your days comfortably.

And we'll say, for the sake of argument, that you will spend the next thirty years paying for college tuition and covering the mortgage and that you have no more money to invest.

> The various asset classes are described in Section 8.

Using a present-value calculator—or clicking into any number of retirement-savings worksheets or calculators offered on countless financial Internet sites—you determine that it will take a return of just over 7 percent annually to turn your current nest egg into your complete retirement cushion.

Now look at the various asset classes and develop realistic expectations of what they can deliver. Most financial professionals base such expectations on data developed by Ibbotson Associates, a Chicago-based investment research firm, which shows that the average annual return on small-company stocks has been 13.2 percent since 1970. It has been 12.8 percent for large-cap stocks, 12.1 percent for international stocks, 9.8 percent for both long-term corporate and government bonds, and 6.8 percent for Treasury bills.

> You can gain historical performance perspective on a wide variety of indexes affecting virtually any realm of the stock market by using data compiled by Frank Russell Company and available at **www.frankrussell.com**

Remember that past performance is no great predictor of the future—T-bills these days are closer to 4.5 percent—so you need to build a portfolio that delivers the necessary return (7-plus percent in our example) with some cushion and security.

Start by seeing if you could live entirely in stocks, divided roughly evenly between large- and small-company stocks and international holdings. This would give you a much better than needed return.

If you would sleep better with some of the money safely tucked into Treasuries and bonds, this lowers the portfolio's return but reduces the likelihood of losses and makes your aim more accurately at the ultimate target.

The role of bonds in your portfolio is to provide stable income and certainty.

As you get closer to the event you are funding—when it is time to make things happen in your financial life—even temporary losses can have severe implications. That's why you cut back on the stocks, giving up the opportunity for bigger gains in exchange for the certainty of bonds.

Remember, too, that how much money you have greatly influences your decision. In our example, if you hit age thirty-five with just half as much ($125,000) in assets, you need a return of more than 10 percent a year. That pushes you more toward stocks.

Conversely, if you are "set for life"—say you already have the $2 million—you could simply protect it with safe investments, a boring but highly effective strategy. Some people set aside what they need—I call this "don't-mess-it-up money"—and put it in money-market accounts or bonds to protect it from market risk. Even when you protect your money, always keep a little something in equities; if interest rates fall dramatically in the future, the safe strategy that looks so good today might look awful in a decade.

> For a breakout on how many funds and what type of funds to own in a diversified portfolio, see Section 27.

> Your job in setting an allocation is to develop a mix that gives you a high sleep factor but also a reasonable probability that it can enable you to reach your target return rate.

A MISTAKE TO AVOID

Following rules of thumb or even the sample portfolios you see in many publications without doing research that applies to your own situation is not a wise approach. "Your age equals the percentage of money you should keep in bonds" may sound nice, but that formula will be wrong for most people.

Rules and suggested portfolios are guidelines. Most newsletter editors I have talked to acknowledge that some people following such sample portfolios could wind up with half of their money in the wrong places.

THE RIGHT WAY TO PROCEED

If you want to test out your current asset allocation and get an idea whether you are on the right track, the best free evaluation on the Internet is available at

www.financialengines.com, a web site developed with guidance from Nobel Prize–winning economist William Sharpe.

The site is trying to sell you financial services, and it has shortcomings—as does any site that bases its assumptions on various rules of thumb—but it also gives you the most complete forum for inputting your current assets and projecting your ability to move ahead.

The forecast, essentially, tells you the likelihood that you will reach your financial goal, as in "There's a 38-percent chance you will save enough to meet your retirement needs."

Study the site carefully and change your forecast to reflect what you might do—the funds you may buy if you need to be more aggressive, for example—so that you get one real, precise forecast and a number of hypotheticals. The results are likely to be scary—I have yet to meet anyone who came away from this program feeling completely certain they were on the right track—but it will give you a good idea of whether your asset allocation works.

DIVERSIFICATION

A FEW YEARS BACK, I GOT A LETTER FROM A MAN who had thirty-six mutual funds and wondered whether he was diversified enough.

That's no misprint. He had thirty-six funds.

It seems he had bought one fund for each of the Morningstar style-boxes (there are nine boxes), and then he wanted to diversify, so he bought a second fund in each box (for a total of eighteen). Then there were nine bond funds—one for each style-box Morningstar assigns for bonds—plus five funds in his 401(k) program, two funds for his IRA, and two more for his wife's IRA.

That's not a portfolio—it's a collection. And it shows how easy it is to amass a collection of funds. You invest here and there over time, keep finding new investment vehicles that look or sound good, change jobs once or twice, fill in the portfolio with funds that cover style-boxes you never pursued before and—Presto!—you've got a fund collection. As my friend Jason Zweig at *Money* magazine likes to put it: "That's not diversification, it's diworsification."

You may be able to explain away how you got so many funds, but that does not excuse having such a mess of funds from an investment standpoint. How many funds an investor owns is a critical issue both in building a portfolio and setting expectations. It is central to the risk-versus-reward trade-off you make when investing.

> The truth is that most investors can accomplish everything they need with anywhere from four to ten funds. Keeping the number of funds small will improve your profitability in the long run.

Too few funds can leave a portfolio undiversified and volatile. Too many issues typically melt into a costly, hard-to-maintain, no-better-than-average lump. Funds are not works of art or collectible baseball cards. Two autographed Mark McGwire baseball cards are twice as valuable as one. But two funds that run in exactly the same style are redundant and self-defeating. Since most funds own more than 100 stocks within their asset class, there's a good chance you will wind up owning the same stocks over and over again, paying the managers to trade the stock from one of your funds to the next.

Reduced returns are the price you pay either for being indecisive or a fund junkie. Virtually all studies—and there have been plenty in this area—show that any four funds in one asset group will combine to form a closet index fund but that anything beyond two funds in an asset class is probably too many.

> Buying too many funds can land you with what the pros call a "closet index fund," where the combined holdings of all funds in one asset group deliver performance that is no better than the index but at a much higher cost.

"More than one manager or investment strategy [per asset type] can be a good idea. But after two or three, you should manage the portfolio and not simply add on," says Mark Stumpp, managing director and chief investment officer for Prudential Diversified Investment Strategies in Newark, New Jersey. "The idea is not to have lots of funds but to have a few funds that do well for you."

For most people, the magic number of funds to own is somewhere between four and ten, depending on circumstances, risk tolerance, and what's available in your retirement plan (where you may have to suffer a few less-than-ideal choices in order to put together a retirement-savings portfolio).

The basic breakdown—one supported by a 1999 study by the Schwab Center for Investment Research—includes diversified equity funds from three different asset classes (large-company, small-company, and international), plus one diversified bond fund. You can double up in an asset class, further diversifying your holdings but also potentially dampening returns, and then you can look to complete your portfolio by delving into other investment categories such as mid-sized and micro-company funds, sector funds, international bond funds, and all the rest that many investors use to flesh out a portfolio.

"If you get beyond ten funds, you need to sit down and say, 'What is the role of each fund? What are these funds doing for me?'" says Mark Riepe, head of Schwab's investment research group. His personal portfolio totals seven funds. "It's not that you can't make a case to own more funds or cut things up more ways, it's that the average investor probably has no reason to hold more, and is probably hurting performance if they do."

Some people don't feel that they are very good at picking funds, so they constantly buy new ones rather than adding to existing holdings in the hope that their next pick will be the right one. Others—those with big accounts—buy many funds because they feel nervous about having a huge chunk of their money in any one fund.

Many fund accumulators buy their funds without concern for their asset allocation, which compounds the problem. They wind up with five funds covering, say, large-company growth stocks but have nothing in other key investment arenas. The end result is synthetic index performance in the area where they are overweighted and less diversification than they think they have overall.

Fund "collectors" also tend to become attached to their funds, the way a baseball fan keeps the cards of a favorite player. The fund has done well for them in the past, they have had it for years, and they develop an emotional attachment that lingers even if performance starts to fade.

Mutual funds are investment vehicles, pure and simple. Personal "favorites" should constantly be redefined by what works to meet investment goals now and in the future. If a different fund in the same asset class looks better to you in the future, you need to question why you are still holding onto the old one. It may be to avoid taxes—a legitimate concern for investors in taxable accounts—but it should not be for emotional or sentimental reasons.

> Holding too many funds is more an emotional decision than a rational one, often emanating from an investor's own insecurities.

If you have more than ten funds, your real challenge lies in managing your portfolio and eliminating overlap. And therein lies the real problem: deciding what to get rid of to slim down your holdings. With funds required to report their holdings only on a semiannual basis, there is no easy way to gauge overlap in a portfolio. Even helpful measures such as Morningstar's style-boxes don't always work; a fund that splits assets in half between large and small stocks would grade out as a mid-cap fund, even though it is not invested that way.

"What is most important is how your funds are the same or different, not how many you own," says Bill Chennault, a computer administrator at Kansas City (Kansas) Community College, who developed Overlap software to determine the degree of duplication between funds. "If two funds overlap a lot, that's one too many for that asset category. You don't add much diversification buying funds that invest the same way."

Start searching for overlap by looking for redundancy when you compare investment objectives and styles and recent portfolio holdings from semiannual reports, or do your search by using a service such as Morningstar, Value Line, or Overlap. Several Web sites—notably Morningstar's and **www.findafund.com**—have functions that allow you to see the crossover between two or more funds.

> Eliminating overlap in your holdings will keep the number of funds down, will increase your portfolio's ability to meet your expectations, and will help you avoid the paperwork monster that comes along with a fund collection.

As Stephen M. Savage, executive editor of the *No-Load Fund Analyst* newsletter, says: "If you have a lot of funds, there is a built-in limitation to what the next fund can accomplish. Once you have a fund or two in the important asset classes, spend your personal research time determining the right mix of assets for you, rather than looking for the fund to add next."

THE RIGHT WAY TO PROCEED

If you have more than 10 funds, get the prospectuses from each and start to compare. See where you have more funds than needed in any given asset class (as well as any asset classes that you want to own but that aren't covered currently).

Wherever two or more funds appear to be doing the same job for you, consider whether there is a good reason to hang on to the weakest of your selections or whether you would be better off consolidating your holdings or redeploying your money elsewhere.

Even if tax burdens keep you from making a change now, earmark the funds that you would like to unload to make your portfolio more efficient. If, for any reason, you need to dip into your holdings in the future, these are the accounts you will want to draw down first.

> *Obsession with broad diversification is the sure road to mediocrity. Most people who own more than two mutual funds are over-diversified.*
> —JOHN NEFF, FORMER PORTFOLIO MANAGER,
> VANGUARD WINDSOR FUND, AND ONE OF
> THE MOST SUCCESSFUL FUND MANAGERS IN HISTORY

27

REBALANCING A PORTFOLIO

WHEN THE WHEELS ON A CAR GET OUT OF ALIGNMENT, the vehicle begins pulling, drifting to the point that you must oversteer to stay on the road and out of accidents. The same goes for investment vehicles. Over time, mutual-fund portfolios tend to slide away from their planned asset allocation and slip out of alignment.

The cause varies. It can be that a mutual fund drifts from one investment style to the next as it grows—and takes your asset allocation along for the ride. It might just be that a certain market segment gets hot (or cold), growing (or shrinking) at a pace that makes it too heavy (or light).

> Being a bit off your asset allocation is not necessarily a problem. It's when you get way off base that you are in for a surprise, potentially having too much of your money exposed to one type of risk. See Section 25 on asset allocation.

To avoid this kind of problem, consider periodically "rebalancing" your portfolio to keep it on course. Rebalancing is particularly important after a strong market move, where one segment of the market surges far ahead of the rest. Rebalancing is ordinary fund maintenance, a defensive, protect-yourself strategy that's easily accomplished but hard to make yourself do. That's because it goes against the adage about "letting winners run and cutting losers."

Rebalancing typically involves trimming winners and putting the gains from the hot stuff into the slower-growth parts of a portfolio, which is precisely why a lot of folks never do it. Putting money into the less productive areas of a portfolio, however, effectively insures that you are "buying low," while pruning your winners allows you to "sell high."

Done too often, however, rebalancing turns into market-timing. That's why a portfolio tune-up every eighteen months to two years should be sufficient in most market conditions.

That mutual-fund allocation strategies get out of whack is actually the natural order of things. Historically, stock investments grow faster than bond purchases; over time, this tendency makes a fund drift toward higher weightings in stocks.

> If you are rebalancing because of current market moves—rather than because your portfolio is not apportioned in accordance to your financial plan—you are timing the market. Calling it a rebalancing doesn't change that fact.

Say, for example, you invested $10,000 around the beginning of 1997, planning to maintain a portfolio that is 75-percent invested in stock funds and 25 percent in taxable bonds.

Over the next three years, your funds were average, meaning the stock funds delivered roughly 20 percent per year, while your taxable bond funds gained 5 percent annually. By the end of 1999, your portfolio had grown to about $16,000, but more than 82 percent of that money—much of it winnings accumulated during the three-year period—was in the stock funds.

That kind of performance spread will shift your allocations by a few percentage points in any given year. Some financial advisers recommend change any time the assets stray as much as 1 percent off the plan—arguing that failing to rebalance lets the market dictate your strategy and strips you of control—but plenty will let things ride for awhile.

In light of that, any time you have moved five to ten points off the plan, it's time for a change.

REBALANCING TECHNIQUES

The actual rebalancing process can be accomplished in four different but easy methods, one of which is available almost exclusively to older investors.

The first is the obvious:

Sell what you need to cut back on.   The drawback here is that your moves could create a tax bill, unless the money being moved around is in a tax-advantaged account. There may also be other charges, such as back-end loads and redemption fees, that are worth considering before moving money around.

If you must move monies around that are currently invested to complete a rebalancing, try to make the changes within your tax-deferred accounts first in order to minimize the possible tax damage you incur from making a change.

The next rebalancing option avoids that problem altogether:

Leave all current monies in place but change where new investments go.   If, for example, you are off your planned asset allocation because you have too much money in large-company stocks—a common malady, given the bull market of the late 1990s—you can rebalance by putting all new investments toward smaller stocks. This way, you get the "buy low" part of the formula without the tax pain that comes from selling high. Over time, as your new investments keep coming in—and this is helped along if the market shifts its focus and out-of-favor issues return to the fore—your portfolio moves back toward the intended asset-allocation target.

You may stop putting money into the hot sector indefinitely; if it keeps out-gaining the other portions of your allocation plan—and your investment strategy does not change—you may never go back to putting additional investments in the hot area.

The third way to rebalance a portfolio works only for people who must remove money from their fund accounts:

Make strategic but necessary withdrawals.   Typically, this applies to older investors, who may be required to take annual distributions from retirement accounts. If rebalancing is an issue, pull the annual distribution from the investments that are the most overweight in your asset-allocation plan.

If the money being withdrawn is not being spent—if you are taking a distribution because it is in the rules, not because you need the money to live—roll the cash into the underweight portions of your asset allocation.

The fourth method is not offered by all fund firms:

Cross-reinvest your dividends and capital gains.   This is a little-known service offered by some fund companies, where the dividends and capital gains paid off by one fund are reinvested into a different fund. In this fashion, instead of rolling over these payments into the overweighted part of the portfolio, they are pulled automatically and invested in the underweight part of your portfolio.

If you are invested with some of the big fund families or the fund supermarkets, you should inquire about cross-reinvesting your dividends and capital gains. See details on page 201.

No matter which method of rebalancing you choose, you should be able to quickly get your portfolio moving back toward your planned allocation. Once there, repeat the process every few years to make sure that your holdings always stay within reach of your up-to-date strategy and plan.

WRONG-WAY SIGNS

Rebalancing is about checking to see if you are on course to meet your goals with the amount and types of risk you are willing to accept. Once outside market forces enter into the equation—where something other than your asset allocation is pushing you toward making a change—you are timing the market rather than fixing an out-of-kilter portfolio.

THE RIGHT WAY TO PROCEED

Check your holdings against your plan, the asset allocation you feel most comfortable pursuing. You may not want to rebalance until the spreads are significant, but knowing where you stand and how your allocations are changing will allow you to keep control of your portfolio even as your winners continue to run.

28
section

MEASURING PERFORMANCE AND BENCHMARKING

IT'S NORMAL TO LOOK AT YOUR FUNDS and wonder "How am I doing?"

And the way you answer that question is crucial, because it may be the key factor in deciding your level of satisfaction with a fund. For example, many investors have expressed disappointment in funds by noting that "90 percent of all actively managed funds failed to beat the Standard & Poor's 500 Index" for much of the 1990s.

That would be a meaningful statistic if all of those funds were trying to match the S&P. But a great percentage of those funds—anything in small-company stocks, international stocks, bonds, emerging markets, most sectors, and so on—aren't aiming at the S&P as a target.

Late in 1999, Morningstar, Inc. president Don Phillips pointed out the flip side of that statistic, which is that 95 percent of all indexes had failed to beat the S&P. That might explain why funds that measure themselves against other benchmarks failed to top the S&P.

IMPORTANT BENCHMARKS

There are three benchmarks that truly matter:

1. How the fund does relative to the proper index. Funds usually show this information in their reports, but they sometimes try to get away with comparing themselves to a less-accurate reflection of what they do.

Common-stock and large-cap funds are properly compared to the S&P or perhaps the Wilshire 5000 Index, which examines the total stock market. Small-cap stocks measure up against the Wilshire 4500 (which kicks out the biggest companies) or the Russell 2000. International stocks go up against the Morgan Stanley Capital International EAFE Index (EAFE stands for Europe, Australasia, Far East). Taxable-bond funds should be measured against the Lehman Brothers Aggregate Bond Index, municipal bond funds against the Lehman Muni Bond Index, and government money-market funds against the Salomon Brothers Three-Month Treasury Bill Index.

> All bond funds should also be compared to inflation, as measured by the consumer price index (CPI).

You can also cut the indices more finely than this—and some fund companies do, especially when it makes for a more favorable comparison—but these are the bogies your funds should most likely be shooting for.

2. How the fund does relative to its peers. Judging a fund solely against an index leaves out some important context, namely, whether some other fund in the same asset category could deliver better returns for you.

Most fund companies will provide the data for the relevant Lipper Index, which is effectively the average performance of all funds in any given asset category. Morningstar's category rating also tells you how the fund stacks up against its direct competition. If your fund does not supply you with this information in statements, it can usually get it for you pretty quickly. Don't be afraid to call the fund to ask for these data (as opposed to finding one of many web sites that might have it on-line), because you could get the number along with some explanation from the phone representative as to what was going on to make performance better or worse than average.

> It is possible for a fund to have a good star rating because its asset class is soaring but to have a poor category rating because every fund in the grouping is doing really well. For more details on fund ratings, see Section 16.

While comparing the fund to its peers, don't forget to see how risk figures into the equation. A fund that looks like a laggard may simply be more conservative than most of the competition. If you bought the fund because you wanted a risk-averse strategy, you should not be quick to punish it for falling behind; returns in up markets are not the only measure of success, and you may have gone with the conservative choice in order to avoid serious downturns. When the market turns around, a more risky fund might be an even bigger laggard.

> Measuring and managing risk is covered in detail in Section 21.

If one of your holdings is consistently trailing its peers and is high risk to boot, chances are that it will fail the benchmark test on all counts. But don't let benchmarking make you lose sight of the collective factors that were involved in your selection of the fund.

3. How the fund is doing relative to your expectations and goals. This is not something you will find in the company's statements, but it is crucial for your investment satisfaction. If you bought a fund expecting a certain return and the fund has met those expectations, there is no reason to be unhappy with the fund even if it has lagged the first two benchmarks.

Set your expectations and plans around reasonable expectations for each category of fund, which means extrapolating some measure of historical returns and projecting them into the future. Some folks argue that you should only consider the long-term return of stocks based on all market history dating back about 100 years (in which case the long-term return on stocks is roughly 10 percent per year). Others would say that the ten most recent years are the relevant ones and that the others are ancient history.

> If you put absolute performance as the first, last, and most-important factor in deciding your happiness with a fund, you are certain to be disappointed on a regular basis and to find yourself running away from funds far too often.

Clearly, the last ten years have been particularly friendly to the stock market, but here are the average annualized returns earned by major fund categories during the 1990s: Large-cap growth stocks earned 20.0 percent annually; small-cap growth, 19.82 percent; international stock funds, 8.62 percent; balanced funds, 11.75 percent; equity-income funds, 12.68 percent; corporate bond funds (A rated), 6.86 percent; general U.S. government funds, 6.37 percent; general municipal debt funds, 6.01 percent.

Obviously, market factors could change expectations for all of these groups (and past performance is no indication of future returns, as every disclaimer properly warns), and it would be better to set expectations below these levels and be pleasantly surprised than to push the limits and wind up unhappy with your funds all the time.

Regardless of which of these three benchmarks you are measuring your fund against, be sure to use "total return" as the measure of your fund's performance. Total return includes price appreciation plus dividends and capital gains, and it is better than simple price appreciation as a means of measuring what the fund really delivered.

> In addition to total return, you also may want to calculate your "dollar-weighted returns in the fund" to get the truest measure of how your money did in the fund over a period.

Total return measures how much a fund's investments have gained or lost over a particular time period, where a fund's share price or net asset value shrinks every time the fund pays out a dividend or capital gain (which is why a fund may have a positive total return even if the share price has been stagnant, just because the share price falls back whenever gains are paid out).

What's more, the most important total return is that of your entire portfolio rather than any individual fund. With each fund added to your holdings for a specific reason, you will have a variety of returns relative to averages, but the biggest question remains whether your overall strategy is getting you where you want to go. If it isn't, the problem may be your asset allocation every bit as much as it is your funds.

THE LEAST YOU SHOULD REMEMBER

The S&P 500 is not the only benchmark, nor is it necessarily the most important index for you to measure performance against. It is simply the index that is most widely quoted as representing "the market."

Forget about the S&P unless it is the appropriate benchmark and add in a comparison of how the fund does versus peers rather than an index.

FIGURING YOUR REAL
PERFORMANCE IN A FUND

WHEN A MUTUAL FUND TOUTS ITS PERFORMANCE, it is telling the world how well it did. It is not necessarily saying how well you did in the fund.

Those two things aren't always the same. How a fund performs for you actually depends on timing, additional investments, capital gains rollovers, withdrawals made during the year, and other factors. In short, if you have a unique flow of funds into an account, your return is unique and is neither what the fund advertises nor what your neighbor might get investing in the same fund. For that reason, a fund's gross returns are less important than the "dollar-weighted returns" in your own account.

Dollar-weighted or time-weighted returns take into account how much money you have in a fund and when that money was invested. Some professionals call this the "internal rate of return" on an investment. For example, in 1999, I owned a fund that was up roughly 5 percent for the year, yet my account actually gained only 3.5 percent.

The difference reflects my behavior as an investor; specifically, it reflects the additional investments I made during the year and the timing of those transactions. (It could have been equally affected by withdrawals, though I did not make any.) Although the difference in this case was narrow, the spread between a fund's performance and your actual results can be huge, particularly if you buy a hot fund just as it begins to cool.

This is how investors wind up with a portfolio of "good funds," but without the good results to show for it.

Back to my fund as the example: By the middle of July, the fund was up more than 17 percent for the year. Any money invested at that high point—and I make automatic monthly deposits—lost more than 10 percent through the end of the year. In fact, almost everything invested in this fund after the start of May wound up the year with a loss. Thus, while most of my money was in the fund for the whole year and finished up 5 percent, my new investments showed a loss.

> There are many times where a hot fund reports a great year but earned all of its gains during the first few months; investors who bought in after the hot streak are showing a loss, but the fund remains positive for the year.

That's the reason that unless you hold a fund all year without making a move in it, your real return is as individual as you are. The more a fund tends to run hot and cold, the more important it is to watch your dollar-weighted returns.

Some fund companies calculate dollar-weighted returns for you, by the way, giving you a personalized portfolio accounting. As more consumers ask for this feature, more fund companies will come into line. Financial advisers should give you this kind of data when they review annual performance (although many do not), and you may be able to do it with a number of personal-finance software packages or web sites. The more precise your data as to exactly when purchases were made, the more accurate the numbers you get back from these sources.

> The best time to examine your dollar-weighted returns is at the end of the year, when your last statement comes in and shows all activity for the fund during the year. Since this is also the best time for an annual review of your investment performance, you can make this exercise part of your fund-evaluation process.

ESTIMATING TIME-WEIGHTED RETURNS

In any account where you simply hold the fund and do not add to it over time, your return will match the fund's stated performance. But estimating your time-weighted returns on funds where you add money regularly or periodically is easy to do on your own. Here's how:

Start with your last statement of the year, which details all of your transactions for the twelve-month period. (If you take out statements for all of your funds, you can aggregate the balance and transaction amounts to estimate the dollar-weighted return of your entire portfolio.)

From the statement, get the following information:

- The balance in your account (or portfolio) at the start of the year. From now on, we'll call this your **starting balance**.
- The value of that account—plus any dividends, capital gains, or interest that you took in cash instead of reinvesting—at year's end. This is your **ending balance**.
- The total value of additional investments, minus any withdrawals, made during the year.

Next, pull out your calculator and do the following:

Step 1. Calculate your **average monthly balance**.   To do this, subtract your starting balance from your ending balance.

Cut the result in half, then add back the amount of your starting balance. The result is the average amount you had in the fund during any month of the year.

Step 2. Calculate your **total gain**.   Add your starting balance to your additional investments (or withdrawals).

Subtract the result from your ending balance, and you have the amount of your gain that is attributable to growth in the fund during the year.

Step 3. Determine your **real return** from the fund.   Divide your total gain by your average monthly balance, and multiply the result by 100.

The result is your total percentage gain for the year—on existing and new investments—before taxes.

It's not perfect. If your new investments were all either early or late in the year, it will skew the numbers. If you invest regularly, however, the results should be accurate. Furthermore, the ups and downs should even out for regular investors over time. But if you find you always buy in at highs and ride out the downturns, consider changing the way you pick funds or the way you decide when the time is right to throw more money at a particular fund.

Investment adviser Michael Stolper of Stolper Asset Management in San Diego says: "Once you have the number [for real returns in your funds], use it responsibly. Compare it to an appropriate benchmark and see if the fund and your investment strategy are meeting your needs over time. That's how these numbers can be most helpful."

THE RIGHT WAY TO PROCEED

Do the math. If your returns in a fund are markedly different from that of the fund, try to identify why that is. The most common reason is that investors make periodic investments, throwing more dollars into whichever fund is hot. The result is that they are always "buying high," which can be a drain on their performance.

If this is the case, consider making automatic periodic (monthly or quarterly) investments into the fund instead of doing lump sums every now and again.

30

FUND SUPERMARKETS AND WRAP ACCOUNTS

ALTHOUGH THIS BOOK IS ABOUT thinking like an owner of mutual funds rather than a purchaser of products, there is one area where it is fine to combine the qualities of the two—convenience.

A growing number of fund investors buy their funds through a "supermarket," a network of unrelated funds marketed together under the label of a brokerage firm. Think of it as the same as buying groceries. In previous times, buying groceries meant stopping at the butcher shop, the greengrocer, the fruit stand, the ice cream shop, and so on. Today, you can still go to those places—or you can get them all under one roof at the supermarket.

Fund supermarkets are a one-stop shopping convenience. Fidelity, Vanguard, and several other big fund firms run their own supermarkets—featuring more funds from other companies than they have on their own—as do most major brokerage firms. Most of the firms in the business operate using a similar model, specifically the one most commonly associated with Charles Schwab and Company.

> Mutual-fund supermarkets let you buy thousands of funds from hundreds of fund families under one roof.

In Schwab's supermarket, you'll find funds for which there is no-load and no transaction fee (NTF) and funds with a load, a transaction fee, or both.

That funds need to "pay for shelf space" in a funds supermarket is the biggest drawback to these systems. The additional costs raise a fund's expenses, which you pay for in the end.

The upside is the ease of managing a portfolio through a supermarket. Instead of contacting half a dozen fund companies and dealing with them individually, you get to set up one account with the supermarket. If you want to buy a new fund, you simply place the order; there is no new application to fill out, no paperwork to handle (although you should still create a record of why you are buying the fund).

> Beware: NTF funds aren't really free because they generally have to pay a fee to be included in the supermarket. Fund companies tend to levy these additional fees on shareholders, so you pay the supermarket price even if you buy a no-load fund directly from the management company.

Your statements are also consolidated into one, which is a big plus come tax time, when you would otherwise be stuck adding up the capital gains and dividends from multiple funds. When you switch funds, your money moves seamlessly and quickly from one fund family to the next, instead of coming to you via check, which you then deposit by mail into the new fund (although electronic banking makes it possible to avoid this kind of time lag).

One other key advantage for supermarkets is that they typically have their own investment minimums. Schwab's, for example, is $2,500 in a fund. That means that if you want a fund that typically has a $25,000-minimum initial investment but you don't have that kind of cash lying around, you can get the fund through the supermarket for as little as $2,500.

Many supermarkets also are set up so that financial advisers can manage client money in a consolidated fashion, and many load funds will waive their sales charges for investments made through advisers participating in a supermarket like Schwab's OneSource. The waived load can be a benefit, although many supermarkets impose redemption charges or restrictions in exchange for waiving up-front fees on funds.

For all of their convenience and ease, supermarkets have their question marks (as does virtually everything in fund investing).

IMPORTANT QUESTIONS

Before picking a supermarket, answer the following questions:

Does the network have the funds I want? If, for example, you want Vanguard funds, you most likely will have to go through Vanguard's network. If it's Fidelity that catches your fancy, you might choose Fidelity's FundsNetwork supermarket. Both of those supermarkets exclude any number of popular fund groups. By comparison, the funds supermarket at Waterhouse Securities has a wider selection, but it is weaker on the Big Two of Schwab and Fidelity.

In short, consider which funds you want to buy now and are likely to want to consider in the future. Drop from consideration any supermarket that doesn't offer those funds.

What does a statement look like? Since a consolidated statement is a big part of the reason for joining a supermarket, look at a sample and make sure you understand everything you are getting and that it's really valuable compared to what you have now.

Supermarkets also let you combine statements not only for your funds but for your stocks, so that you can examine all investments on one paper. If you are a stock investor and want to move your holdings into the supermarket system, make sure you compare the network's stock capabilities to what you get from your current broker.

What is the fee structure? You will be looking at an annual fee, in addition to the possibility of paying heightened expenses on funds that participate in the NTF system. Then there will be charges if you decide to buy funds outside of the network (you can buy those funds directly, but that ruins the one-statement convenience that was a big part of your reason for making this move).

Some supermarkets have a system that lets you buy load funds directly from other investors, avoiding the sales charge in exchange for paying what amounts to a matchmaker fee. This can represent a big savings off a sales load, but only if you are making reasonably big trades and working with a reasonable fee structure.

What kind of research materials are available, and at what cost?   Some supermarkets provide quarterly performance rankings of funds they offer, while others provide one-page reports from firms like Morningstar. Some provide materials or newsletters on their funds at an extra charge.

> See if the supermarket puts a limit on the number of free trades you get. If it does, find out how many swaps you can make for free and what the cost will be if you exceed that limit.

You may not need the supermarket for its research capabilities, but you probably should know what's available and pursue a network that provides you with meaningful information when you request it.

How do I interact with the network?   This is about your lifestyle. If you are a night owl but you still like to talk to a real person, chances are you will want one of the larger networks that offers service representatives around the clock. If you want to be able to meet brokerage officials face-to-face, you likely will choose between Schwab and Fidelity since they have the biggest branch systems, but you might choose the network from a smaller firm that has an office or service representative in your town.

If you intend to do most of your investing via the computer, check out the web sites you will be dealing with for ease of use and navigation.

A different type of one-stop shopping for funds is something called the "wrap account." As the name suggests, a wrap account bundles investments and services together for a single fee, with the whole portfolio managed by a financial adviser or money manager.

Many firms now offer wrap accounts on investments of as low as $25,000, which is dramatically lower than the minimums usually charged by big money-management firms (which frequently start at $500,000 or more). In fact, some financial advisers charge wrap fees for investing your money in a specific supermarket; the difference is that they have control over your money.

The idea here is that you get professionally managed fund selections plus ongoing portfolio review and rebalancing, monthly or quarterly account statements, and various fund-trading and transaction-cost benefits. Generally speaking, load-fund companies waive their sales charges for wrap customers, who are paying an average fee of 1.5 percent or more to the adviser who is overseeing the account.

Ultimately, that fee represents the biggest drawback to wrap accounts. You not only pay the management fee of the adviser who picks the funds but the expense ratios of the funds themselves. And though you might get the load waived, you also pay the extra management fee every year.

So, let's say a wrap account charges 1.5 percent of assets under management as its annual fee. If it saves you a 3-percent up-front sales charge, it's a bargain for the first two years. That time frame doubles if the waived load is closer to 6 percent. (During that period, you also have more money invested than if you subtracted a whole load up front.)

For most people motivated enough to read a book like this, wrap accounts will not be the answer. But if you find the idea appealing and useful, get answers to the following questions before signing up:

- How much is the annual wrap fee, and is it negotiable?
- Are all sales loads and transaction costs included?
- Are there any extra costs, redemption fees, termination fees, or other possible expenditures beyond the wrap fee and fund costs?

> If you are expecting to be a lifetime investor in the funds you own, the wrap fee becomes very expensive over the long haul and may change your thinking on how best to manage.

- What funds are available in the wrap program?
- What specific services do I get for my money?
- How will the account be managed? How will decisions to change funds or asset allocations be made?

Having run a wrap program through these questions—and having reviewed fund supermarkets—you can decide which issues are most important to you and whether you want to participate and cut your fund shopping down to one stop or whether you want to continue investing directly on your own.

SOMETHING TO CONSIDER

As funds continue to develop their Internet presence, you may not need a fund supermarket to do one-stop shopping, as your only necessary stop could be your own computer and a few benchmarks. Check out the web sites for your fund company and see if there are any portfolio-tracking web sites that would allow you to consolidate statements with little effort. You may be able to give yourself virtually everything a supermarket offers.

THE RIGHT WAY TO PROCEED

If you are interested in fund supermarkets, you probably will want to call some of the largest for information on their programs. Here are the toll-free phone numbers for some of the major players in the funds supermarket business:

AccuTrade, 800-882-4887
Fidelity FundsNetwork 800-544-9697
Charles Schwab, 800-266-5623
Muriel Siebert and Company, 800-872-0444
Vanguard FundAccess, 800-992-8327
TD Waterhouse, 800-233-3411

PAYING TAXES ON YOUR FUNDS

ONE OF THE MOST CONFUSING ASPECTS of fund ownership involves taxes, specifically paying and accounting for them. Such taxes and their accounting can be such bother that they are the main reason some investors—usually those with a lot of money to invest and a need to control their tax exposure—avoid funds altogether.

Here's why: Funds have two choices when it comes to the capital gains and dividends it earns. The fund can pass along these payments to you, its shareholder—which makes you responsible for paying the taxes on the payouts—or it can pay the tax bill itself.

Needless to say, fund companies aren't so magnanimous that they take the second option.

By law, therefore, a fund must distribute virtually all of the capital gains and dividends it accrues in a year. Capital gains, of course, represent profits from the fund's trading activities. Therefore, if the fund buys a stock and sells it for a quick profit, that gain is taxable. If the fund has more gains than losses, it passes the money along to shareholders.

> Even if you buy tax-efficient funds, you will find that taxes are a headache.

Whether that money comes as a check or gets reinvested in the fund, you owe taxes on it (unless the fund is held in an individual retirement account, 401(k) plan, or other tax-deferred account). Dividends, interest, and short-term gains are taxed at your ordinary income-tax rate; gains on stocks the fund holds over a year face a maximum federal rate of 20 percent.

Typically, investors don't connect gains with taxes due. Investors receive a check or see their pile of shares grow when gains are passed out. Since they aren't withholding monies for taxes, they only realize the tax implications later.

Here's how that happens:

Let's say you put $1,000 into a fund at the start of last year. At the end of the year, your statement showed an account worth $1,250, for a pre-tax total return of 25 percent.

> As Securities and Exchange Commission chairman Arthur Levitt has noted on several occasions: "Taxes are one of the most significant costs of investing in mutual funds."

But if $200 of that growth was generated from the fund's short-term trading activity, you will likely lose $60 or more to the government. That lowers the after-tax growth to a maximum of $190, or 19 percent.

That difference may not be enough to make you want to sell a fund, but it illustrates how taxes eat away at returns. It's also why some funds, in tough times for the market, actually may lose money but still pay out gains that give you a tax headache.

> Several studies have shown that for investors in the highest tax bracket, taxes eat up about 2.5 percentage points a year from the return of the average stock fund.

One obvious way to avoid this problem is to buy funds that are tax efficient. But no matter how efficient your fund, you will still have to contend with at least the occasional payout.

With that in mind, you need to know how gains work. Here are the basics: Assume you invest $1,000 in the XYZ Fund on Monday. At the time, the fund's net asset value (NAV) is $25, so you are buying forty shares. On Tuesday, the fund makes a $5-per-share distribution, so it owes you $200 ($5 multiplied by your forty shares). The fund's net asset value—which was inflated by the amount of gains and income it had realized—shrinks by the $5 per share.

> See Section 19 for details on tax-efficient mutual funds.

Presuming you reinvest the fund's payout, your $200 buys you ten more shares. The end result is that you have the exact same $1,000 invested in the fund after the payout that you had before. The only difference is the number of shares in your account and the current net asset value, plus the little statement sent to you and the Internal Revenue Service declaring the $200 payout. (If you do not reinvest your gains or dividends, you have forty shares at $20 each, for an $800 investment, plus the $200 distribution check that was reported to the IRS.)

One of the most common misconceptions investors have about their funds occurs after a gains payout, when shareholders who have not read statements wind up expressing shock or outrage over a fund where net asset value dropped $5 in a single day. Almost always, the move is a distribution that the shareholder missed.

> Investors who don't understand how distributions work have a real problem tracking them for future tax purposes.

Because you pay taxes on distributions you get today, they affect your cost basis in a fund (the amount you paid to buy your shares).

This is crucial when you someday go to sell the fund.

If the XYZ Fund goes up to $50 per share and then you decide to sell, your fifty shares are now worth $2,500. Your initial investment was $1,000, so it would be easy to believe that your taxable gain would be $1,500.

That's wrong.

You bought forty shares at $25, so your initial investment was $1,000. Then, as a result of the rollover, you bought ten more shares at $20 each, for an additional investment of $200. That means your profit in the fund is really just $1,300.

This means that paying taxes on your gains now reduces your gains later (though I don't know of many people who prefer to pay taxes now when they could put them off). In addition, if you fail to properly account for those gains—and many

> To minimize your taxes when you sell the fund—especially if you plan to sell only a part of your stake—keep accurate records showing the dates and amounts of additional investments.

fund families now give shareholders "average-cost accounting" that calculates the average cost paid per share—you could wind up paying taxes on the distribution twice.

To manage the current tax bill on your funds, consider calling the fund company late in the year, when many firms typically prepare estimates of how much per share they are likely to distribute before year's end.

Although these estimates often vary widely from the actual figure—in the mid-1990s, Fidelity estimated a huge gain for its Magellan Fund, only to find a math error that caused it to change the estimated payout to zero—they should give you a ballpark figure to work with when it comes to preparing your tax return. Armed with that number, you can increase withholdings, pay estimated taxes, set aside cash reserves for tax-filing day, or sell off some losers to offset the gains in your funds. The important thing is not to be caught unaware that a fund is about to make a big payment that will put you on the hook with Uncle Sam a few months hence.

When your fund sends your tax documents, be sure to keep the supporting paperwork. Many states have rules for how they tax in-state holdings versus out-of-state stocks, and your fund company will tell you which part of your gain falls within your state's requirements (if any). This could save you a few bucks come tax season.

Over time, as you measure the performance of your funds, factor in their tax efficiency so that you use after-tax figures to see whether a fund is meeting your expectations. A few fund companies now put their after-tax returns up on the company web site, but a bill was pending as this book went to press that would require fund companies to disclose the after-tax performance of their funds in the future.

Even if the law does not pass, don't be shy about calling your fund companies to ask them to help you calculate the after-tax gains you generated in any given year. Over time, if a fund's tax burden dampens returns to a disappointing level, you are likely to want to make a change to a more tax-efficient offering that makes this major headache of fund ownership a little easier to bear.

THE RIGHT WAY TO PROCEED

Every November 1, contact your fund company to find out when gains estimates will come out and when gains will be paid. (Bond funds typically maintain a regular schedule of income payments, but it's still worth getting a handle on the estimated gains for the year.)

Armed with these data, be sure you have set aside enough money to cover the tax burden.

WRONG-WAY SIGNS

If all of your tax-efficient funds are in tax-deferred accounts but you have tax-heavy funds outside of your retirement plans, you've invested backward. If you love a particular high-tax fund, put it in a retirement account where taxes don't dilute performance and leave the tax-efficient offerings for taxable accounts where they can ease your pain.

WHEN A FUND CLOSES
OR REOPENS

It's human nature to want things that we can't have or to treasure those things we have that others might not be able to get. So it is when mutual funds close to new investors.

As a shareholder, a fund closing tends to be good news—it protects the interests of current shareholders and shows that fund management is willing to forgo some potential profits that could be earned by taking in more cash in exchange for staying true to the fund's mission. Alas, as with anything else in the fund business, fund closings and reopenings can also be used as a gimmick, one that capitalizes on human nature to the detriment of the investors/suckers it reels in.

> A fund that is **closed to new investors**, as discussed here, is not the same as a **closed-end fund**.

Funds stop taking new investors or new cash for several reasons. Some do this to pursue an investment discipline that would be disrupted by too much cash, others because they don't want to overburden analytical and support staff, and some because they lack magical opportunities or don't like the look of the market. Fund companies may not be able to process a prolonged influx of money. Or their investment strategy might call for capping the fund to remain maneuverable.

To a potential buyer, a fund that announces it is closing is singing a siren song—the investor must make a quick decision to either get into the popular fund or risk missing out forever. When faced with this situation, chances are you will be better off simply passing and buying something else. To an existing owner, however, the reasons a fund is closing and the way the closing is handled are both worth evaluating—because they may make the fund less attractive in time.

Funds can, and do, close without giving any warning to shareholders in order to prevent any last-minute rush of cash into the fund. If management is having a hard time coping with cash today, turning off the spigot is the most effective way to bring things under control.

Then there are funds that plan to close when they reach a certain asset size, largely because management believes it will be less effective if it gets too far past it. These funds—and the n/i Numeric Investors funds in the late 1990s used this strategy successfully—tend to issue a warning when they near the target zone. They may even give a date when a closing would be likely based on asset flows; as word of the impending door slam gets out, inflows typically increase and the fund may wind up returning monies sooner than anticipated.

> Some funds close without any warning whatsoever; others advertise the date and conditions under which they will close to investors.

The worst type of closing is one that effectively puts the fund on sale as if it were a product available "for a limited time only." In this scenario, a popular fund can draw billions of dollars in before it finally shuts the door, money that may change the character and ability of the fund to deliver on what it has promised, particularly if the fund built its reputation on buying small stocks.

Closings also vary based on the attitude and action of the fund company. Numeric, for example, not only closed to new investors, but it shut down existing shareholders. That meant that shareholders with accounts could not invest more until the funds reopened. By comparison, when Fidelity closed the popular Magellan Fund in the late 1990s, it allowed current shareholders (and investors for whom Magellan was a choice in their retirement plan) to keep investing. Given that about 80 percent of the fund's money was in retirement accounts, the closing actually shut out only a small percentage of the investors who were likely to be interested in the fund.

The key for shareholders/owners in a fund that is closing is to listen to the reasons for the move and to watch what happens to assets in the fund while the fund is going through the lockdown. If assets remain stable and management's reasons for closing seem to protect investors, there is nothing to fear. But studies have shown that funds tend to falter a bit once they close, especially when they take on a lot of new cash at the end.

Knowing the reasons for a closing is crucial because there almost always is a flip side to these stories—the day a fund reopens. At those times, you want to hear a story that makes sense given what management said when the fund closed and what has happened in the stock market since.

> Generally, funds reopen under the guise of "new opportunities in the market." Sometimes that translates into "chances for the fund sponsor to rake in more money."

Reopened funds highlight the conflict of interest inherent in the purchase of any fund. You invest hoping the fund will be managed in your best interest, but the fund is managed for the benefit of its managers. The more money they get in the fund, the more they make, often regardless of whether they can sustain performance while managing a bigger asset pool.

There are no statistics on how funds perform after reopening, but funds that do unlock their doors often do so after a period of poor performance.

For existing shareholders, a reopening looks smart if the fund has little cash and big profits on the stocks it holds. These unrealized gains are a potential tax liability; new blood in the fund inherits this burden and lessens your load.

> A closed fund that opens to take in more cash to pursue new investment opportunities is doing its job; a fund that reopens for the cash alone is just being greedy.

The new cash might also enable the manager to maneuver more efficiently, pursuing new opportunities without jettisoning old ones. Existing shareholders also want money coming in during market downturns, when new cash stabilizes a fund against redemptions.

Shareholders need to critically examine a reopening to see what has changed about the fund or market that makes the opening the right move. Prospective buyers need to be careful that they aren't buying a fund whose legend is greater than its potential, Also find out if management plans to close the fund again after a certain amount of assets come over the transom.

A fund that reopens when it has lost money and other shareholders have fled—especially if its chosen market sector appears to be out of favor and true buying opportunities are scarce—is really doing investors a disservice. Just when management needs to be focused on how to do the best with the money of shareholders who have been hurt by its downturn, it's out trying to pump up the value of its management fees.

"To close a fund . . . means retarding revenue growth [to the fund sponsor] to protect current shareholders," says G. Edward Noonan of Triad Investment Advisory in Hingham, Massachusetts. "If they needed to protect me when they shut down, I'd want to know why they feel it's okay to stop now—how they can handle more money and still maintain performance—or I'd be nervous."

THE LEAST YOU SHOULD REMEMBER

A closing that is structured so that lots of investors can beat the deadline and get into the fund may attract so much money that the fund is changed forever.

And funds that reopen may be motivated more by their own greed than by the idea that it's good for you.

These moves are always talked about as if the fund company is acting benevolently toward shareholders; that's not always the case.

Good funds close with a plan, reopen with a plan, and have some idea of when or why they will close again. It's when the fund doesn't seem to have any plan other than to make a lot of money for management that you really need to worry.

—RUSSELL KINNEL, DIRECTOR OF FUND ANALYSIS
AT MORNINGSTAR, INC.

WHAT'S A NAV?

ONE OF THE FASTEST WAYS TO START AN ARGUMENT over fund investing is to say that a fund's price is no object, that its price is a completely contrived number.

Now I've done it.

Because most investors gauge how well they are doing by how much the fund's share price has increased, they lose sight of the fact that the fund's net asset value is arguably the most meaningless bit of data around. Price, in fact, is such a non-item that it should never factor into your decision to buy a fund (and it won't if you use the methods laid out in this book). If it's not important when buying the fund, it's not going to be too important when you own the fund, either.

That said, you should know what you are looking at when you see a fund's NAV and understand how the number is calculated. The formula is simple enough. Simply tally everything the fund owns, subtract anything it owes, and divide the result by the number of outstanding shares. When you have finished, you have the value of holdings per share, or net asset value (NAV).

> All investors should understand the process of valuing a fund per share, which is the same as calculating the net asset value.

The vast majority of funds trade only at their closing NAV. If you buy or sell a fund at 10 A.M., for example, you get the price at the end of the day. (This could change as the stock markets move toward round-the-clock trading days, although I suspect most firms will still price their funds just once each day.)

Funds start the pricing process in the morning, tallying the previous day's transactions, monitoring the fund's dividend and interest activity, taking an appropriate slice to cover operating expenses, settling trades, adding in the interest, and so forth, all just to get to the point where the market closes and the prices on their current holdings can be calculated.

Fund accountants track prices to four or five decimal places. The difference between $10.0048 and $10.0051 is one penny per share, thanks to rounding. That $10.0051 becomes $10.01; with millions of shares to account for, those pennies add up.

Final prices on specific securities come in from various data providers around 4:15 P.M., leaving less than ninety minutes to determine the fund's closing price and report it to the National Association of Securities Dealers (NASD) for distribution to the media.

Here is where things get tricky. Some funds have hundreds of holdings. And although it usually is easy to value something on the New York Stock Exchange, it can be tricky to value a security from, say, Hong Kong. And bonds must be priced by hand, meaning that the fund accountant has to make a determination of what the bond would be worth if it were sold today. In addition, each fund sets its own rules in its prospectus for how it is going to price certain issues and the lengths to which it will go to "derive the fund's fair value in good faith."

That last bit is important, particularly with esoteric funds that own exotic or unusual securities. For example, the dreaded American Heritage Fund—one of the worst funds ever—has a big chunk of its portfolio tied up in private stock, notably in one particular company that is not traded on any exchange. Effectively, the price of that holding can go for days or weeks without changing because it is not traded by anyone. But if that company suffers an earnings disappointment, the stock can drop precipitously; in one such instance, the fund lost over 10 percent of its value in a single day because it had to reprice the private stock.

Unusual valuation rules notwithstanding, the accountant must price every security to come up with a NAV by 5:40 P.M. Missing that NASD deadline—it gets pushed back on days when the market goes berserk—means the fund's price will be listed as unavailable in the newspaper the next day.

Finally, the fund rechecks the price and sends the legally binding price to the transfer agent, the firm that processes shareholder trades. That's usually, but not always, the same price you see in the paper. Industry statistics show that the numbers in the newspapers are correct more than 99.7 percent of the time. "Not availables" count as errors. The price given to transfer agents is right nearly 99.9 percent of the time.

Which brings us back to whether that price means anything or not.

From the standpoint of an investor who bought a fund at $10 and has seen it go to $15, it certainly does represent a profit. But the exact same fund could just as easily have been priced at $30 per share and could have gone to $45.

Whereas stocks trade based on market sentiment and may be worth more or less than the underlying value of the company, funds trade entirely based on the worth of their holdings. (Closed-end funds, however, trade like stocks and may sell at a premium or a discount.)

Rather than reflecting market sentiment, the price is an arbitrary number picked by the fund family when it started the fund. Say two funds start with $50 million in assets each, one issuing 5 million shares at $10, the other 10,000 shares at $5,000 each. If both funds earn a 10-percent return, investors are rewarded equally. The $10 share hits $11; the $5,000 share grows to $5,500. And $10,000 invested in either fund is now worth $11,000.

The $5,000 share price is outrageously high and the $500 price swing looks steep, but the returns and volatility are exactly the same as if the fund were priced at $10 per share.

Either way, the investor is up 10 percent, which is why the specific share price of the fund is meaningless. All that truly matters is the total return (price appreciation plus distributed capital gains and dividends) in the account.

For proof, consider three Standard & Poor's 500 Index funds that opened within a few weeks of each other in 1990. According to Morningstar, Inc., Vanguard Institutional Index, Fidelity Spartan Market Index, and T. Rowe Price Equity Index each gained roughly 17.5 percent annually from inception through the end of 1999.

At that time, however, the Vanguard fund traded at roughly $116 per share, the Fidelity fund at $88 and the T. Rowe Price fund at $35.

That's three funds, three identical portfolios and strategies, three nearly identical returns (differences due to expense ratios over time), and yet three completely different price points.

What that tells you is that each company picked a different price per share at which to start the fund. It also shows that the share price did not affect the annual rates of return. Since a fund is not priced based on investor sentiment and, since an investor's ability to buy in revolves around the fund's minimum investment requirements rather than the ability to buy a big chunk of shares, this means that share splits are also meaningless. That's why funds don't split their shares often, with only about a dozen funds per year making such a move in the 1990s. Occasionally, a fund will split for cosmetic reasons, for the chance to look more affordable and to appeal to investors' naïveté concerning fund pricing, but that should not be taken by investors as a signal of anything (unlike in stocks, where many experts forecast a rise after a split, simply because it can make a popular stock more affordable for the masses).

> There is no "right" answer for how often to check your funds' prices. Whereas scouring the information daily can lead to panic, not looking enough can leave you unaware that a fund has headed south.

Now that you know what goes into fund pricing, you can see why it's not necessarily advisable to watch your fund's performance each day. When you see big fluctuations in your fund's share price, you are likely to want to act, even though you have no real idea of what caused the move. Since most funds only reveal their holdings sporadically—and the data usually is outdated by the time they are released—you can only guess at what is actually in the portfolio.

Being a long-term investor protects you from what you don't know, so that you don't erroneously interpret the daily fluctuations of a fund and feel a compelling need to "do something" that turns out to be a mistake. The more volatile the assets the fund buys, the more anxiously you should track prices, just to be sure you want to remain invested in the asset class.

But don't sweat it if you look at your fund and see an issue that appears to be priced way above or below the norm. Your concern should never be the price per share, but rather whether management can keep producing the results that attracted you in the first place, buying stocks that push net asset value up even further.

THE LEAST YOU SHOULD REMEMBER

Mutual funds are the one time in your life where you don't have to be rich to say: "Price is no object."

YOUR FUND'S PAPERWORK

As a MUTUAL-FUND INVESTOR, you pay the fund's cost for sending out annual reports, prospectuses, and other informative material. If you don't read these legal documents when they arrive, you are wasting your own money, not to mention missing out on the opportunity to get an update on what's happening inside and around your fund.

In the late 1990s, the Securities and Exchange Commission made a push for more readable, plain-English documents from fund companies. As a result, some of the paperwork you'll receive is no longer written in the somniferous, unintelligible style of years past. This is not to say that the documents are thrillers, just that you can get the information you need without dozing off, provided you know where to look.

Here is a guide to the various documents (excluding your self-explanatory account statements) that you can expect—or ask to receive—from your fund and what to look for in each.

PROSPECTUSES

A prospectus is part operating manual, part contract. Technically, the prospectus is the legal document that tells you what the fund intends to do; when you complete an application, you are agreeing to live with the terms and conditions the fund has laid out in its prospectus.

Once you own the fund, however, the prospectus remains the most telling document you have on a fund (which is why you keep the most current one in your file on the fund, along with the prospectus that initially sold you the fund).

> A prospectus needs careful scrutiny before you buy the fund, so that you can properly determine whether the fund's objectives, risks, and so on meet your needs.

Some fund firms will send you a slimmed down or simplified prospectus—usually as an up-front sales tool—designed to answer key questions about the fund. The good news on these documents is that they are easier to read and give average investors a better chance of understanding the fund they buy. The bad news is that if the investor misunderstands anything, it will be the legalese on the full-blown prospectus that management uses as a defense.

Aside from fund basics on how to open an account, minimum investment requirements, and other boilerplate, the prospectus covers five key elements. They are:

1. Investment objective and strategy.   Near the front of every prospectus, the fund firm lays out its goals and its strategy for achieving those goals. A stock fund, for example, might "seek to maximize capital appreciation by investing principally in large-company and blue-chip stocks."

Investment objectives help you determine whether the fund does what you want it to do—whether it seeks growth, income, safety, and so forth. Be warned, however, that objectives are notoriously and intentionally vague, which is why you will want to look deeper into the prospectus for a heading like "Investment Policies" or simply "Strategies." This is where the prospectus details the types of stocks, bonds, or other securities the fund plans to invest in. Stock funds spell out the types of company they pursue, such as *companies with continued positive earnings growth* or *small, fast-growing firms.* Bond funds lay out the types of bonds they can hold, such as Treasuries, municipals, or corporates.

If the fund can invest overseas, that will be listed here, too. If there are assets the fund can *not* invest in, they'll be specified (and might also be mentioned in the fund's Statement of Additional Information, or SAI).

2. Risks.   This is my favorite part of the prospectus because it tells you what could potentially go wrong. This section generally specifies what can occur if the stock or bond market goes into a decline or how dangerous it is to be investing in an esoteric asset class. The idea here is to "tell you so," so that if problems arise later and you decide to sue, the fund can wave the prospectus and say, "We told you so." It's a disclaimer of sorts.

With that in mind, read this section of the prospectus carefully to make sure you understand all of the dangers involved in holding the fund.

> Funds don't always have to abide by the prospectus. Funds that are named for a specific asset class—such as real estate or technology—need to keep only 65 percent of their assets in that category to comply with SEC rules.

3. Costs. A table near the front of every prospectus makes it easy to determine the cost of one fund compared to another. You can also compare later prospectuses to the one you read when you opened the account, to see how costs have changed over time. The table shows the fund's fees in percentage terms and in absolute dollars, based on a small, standard return. You'll also see the impact of any applicable sales charges.

4. Past performance. The prospectus also contains a chart showing year-by-year gains or losses against a benchmark. If the fund does not have a long history, compare its performance to that of a peer fund with a longer record to help shape expectations for the kinds of returns you might expect from the asset class over time.

5. Management. Funds don't always list the name of the manager—sometimes preferring to simply describe the manager as "team"—but this is the place to look to be certain that the man or woman whom you read so much about is really running the fund.

> If the prospectus names the manager, examine his or her tenure running the fund, as well as any funds this person has run in the past.

If the managers are not listed here, you can usually get more information from the Statement of Additional Information or by calling the fund company and asking.

Remember that a fund is under no legal obligation to tell you when it changes managers, so you will want to check this information every time you get a new prospectus just to see whether there have been any changes at the top.

STATEMENTS OF ADDITIONAL INFORMATION

In 1983, the SEC separated the prospectus into two parts, the first containing essential data on the fund and the second filled with more detailed information. The Statement of Additional Information is part 2 of the prospectus.

An SAI contains a lot of interesting but not essential data, which is why funds are not required to send it out to owners and prospective shareholders unless it is requested. Most transfer agents estimate that fewer than one-half of 1 percent of all shareholders ever request an SAI.

> The SAI is best looked at in comparison with the prospectus. After all, the stuff you **need** to know is in the prospectus, but the SAI contains the stuff you may just **want** to know.

An SAI discloses how much your funds paid in brokerage fees last year, who the directors are, and how much they get paid to sit on the board (and how big a bonus they receive for actually attending a meeting). It's where you find out how the fund divvies up the money it brings in as 12b-1 sales and marketing fees and where you get the skinny on shareholder voting rights.

Here's how the two documents compare:

Prospectus: Basic strategy and risks.
   SAI: Any and all strategies the fund could ever use—no matter how unlikely—
      plus their risks.
Prospectus: Lists fund costs and fees.
   SAI: Shows how those charges are calculated and how the money is spent.
Prospectus: Shows performance.
   SAI: Describes how that performance was calculated.
Prospectus: Names the fund's investment adviser and manager and the basis for
      their compensation.
   SAI: Lists directors and how much they get paid.

If you want an SAI, call the fund company or check out its web site. If you can't get it there for some reason, check out the SEC's web site (www.sec.gov) and root around in the database for filings from the fund. Although funds do not have to send SAIs to shareholders who do not request them, they must file the document with their statements to the SEC.

PROXY STATEMENTS

The proxy is where you find out what your fund wants to do next—because it needs your approval to proceed. All dramatic changes in investment style and strategy must go through shareholders for their agreement. That said, receiving a proxy should put you on alert that a change is coming and that it may not be positive.

By proxy, a fund may be asking to change structure or to give the manager more leeway for the future. You should take note if they want the option to do something that seems out of character, such as adding risky securities to a safe, fixed-income portfolio.

Funds—unlike stocks—aren't required to issue proxies every year, so the mere presence of one should alert you that something is up. Investors whose shares are held in a brokerage or supermarket account may never get the proxy paperwork if their broker is empowered to vote on routine business matters.

Typically, a fund needs to get votes representing half of its outstanding shares; two-thirds of that response pool is needed to approve a change. If too many shareholders ignore their proxy ballots, the fund may hire a firm to collect the vote by phone. If you get a call from a proxy solicitor, don't be pressured into voting until you understand the amendments being proposed.

> Expect all proxy proposals to pass—because failures are extremely rare.

In short, vote your proxies when they arrive; if you don't and you get called by a solicitor, do not vote unless you clearly understand the issue. If you don't, abstain from voting so that you don't push the vote to a conclusion that your fellow shareholders may not want.

Larry Soderquist, director of the Vanderbilt University Corporate and Securities Law Institute and author of *The Investor's Rights Handbook:* "When the management asks for your opinion—and that doesn't happen every day—you must first decide if you can live with the changes being proposed. Otherwise, you could wake up one day and have a very different fund. If you get a call telling you that the fund needs your vote, that should be a wake-up call that it's time to see what is going on with your fund."

ANNUAL AND SEMIANNUAL REPORTS

These documents give you a look at the fund's key information and should paint a picture of whether the fund is acting the way you expected it to when you first bought it.

The key elements to look for in a fund's annual report are:

> After you review one fund, examine the holdings of your funds collectively to see whether your portfolio suffers from overlap—which increases volatility—or has gaps, such as no small-company exposure.

Performance.   Funds must compare returns to at least one benchmark, either the particular market index they try to beat or the average performance of peer funds. Good annual reports show both. Look for reasons that the fund has beaten or lagged those benchmarks; the fund might be shooting for reduced risk and average performance, or its management could be blundering.

Statements from management.   There are just one or two times in a year when your fund manager communicates directly with you, the share owner, on strategy and gives you his or her outlook for the fund and the market. Expect a candid, clear explanation of what happened to the fund, what to expect, and why.

Management's statement should answer questions that any normal, curious shareholder would have, such as why a fund's performance was lackluster or why it experienced a volatile year or how its strategy is likely to do going forward. If all you get is "Don't worry, be happy," get nervous and angry.

The fund portfolio.   Out of date by the time you read the semiannual report, the fund's "Schedule of Investments" still holds clues to strategy and performance. You don't need to scour and research this list—if you were going to work that hard, you could buy the stocks on your own without a fund—but scan the list to make sure the fund's portfolio is consistent with your expectations in terms of diversification, exposure to certain asset classes, and size of companies. A small-company fund, for example, should not have a lot of big-name stocks in it. A portfolio concentrated in a few stocks or one or two industries will be more volatile than a more-diversified counterpart; there is nothing wrong with volatility, so long as it is not unexpected.

Changes in the fund's management or organization. Most funds do not notify shareholders of a manager change until the annual report following the change (obviously, such changes may be in the news, but it's easy to miss a small announcement about a fund). If there has been a change, call for performance details from the new manager's previous funds; your fund will tend to pick up the characteristics of those funds, so make sure you can stomach that strategy.

Expenses and portfolio turnover. Numbers in the "Financial Highlights" can be revealing, but you are more likely to find cost data that you can understand in the fund's prospectus rather than its annual report.

Asset growth. Another number usually found in the financial data, this can be telling. For example, if a fund hasn't grown at all or if it is losing money, investors, or both, that is not a trend you want repeated annually. It also bears watching if it has grown dramatically, because some investment styles seem to fade once they get weighed down with too much money.

The auditor's report. Don't bother trying to read this—it's not one of the sections that has been recast into plain English. Instead, just count the paragraphs; if there are more than three or four, there could be an accounting problem worth further investigation.

THE RIGHT WAY TO PROCEED

At the very least, familiarize yourself with these fund documents. Skim them when they arrive and remember to file current copies. If you'd prefer to receive your documents electronically, inquire whether the fund company offers document delivery by e-mail.

SOMETHING TO CONSIDER

Among the changes you might find in the fund's prospectus or annual report is a switch in transfer agents. The transfer agent is the firm that processes payments and oversees accounts, and the business is so competitive that some funds (especially smaller ones) change every few years.

When you receive statements, look on the envelope that accompanies them (for you to return an account application or additional investment) for the transfer agent's address. If the address has changed, make note of this in your file and toss the old envelopes. Should you send your money to the fund's former transfer agent by mistake, the deposit won't be made and you will need to rectify the error.

HOW YOUR FUND GROUP CAN MAKE YOUR LIFE EASIER

THERE ARE PLENTY OF THINGS IN LIFE THAT WE CAN'T FIGURE OUT.

Many people can't program their VCR properly. My problem is our kitchen stove: I keep hitting the wrong buttons and somehow setting it to measure temperatures on the Celsius scale (which means that I am asking it to be roughly as hot as the sun when I want to broil a steak). My wife knows that the "sleep" feature on our television works, it just never seems to work for her.

In short, many people settle for being able to do the basics, but they leave anything they perceive as complicated or unnecessary alone. In fund investing, that's a shame, because many fund companies have developed features that make investing easier and safer. Yet whenever I talk to fund executives and the firms that implement new systems, they say that the vast majority of investors never bother to participate beyond the most simplistic of services—an automatic investment plan or telephone redemptions; they believe most shareholders don't really know what's out there.

> If you intend to invest in funds for the rest of your life, you might as well make it as easy as possible, and your fund company has features that can help.

Although not every one of these services is available from all fund firms, you can get most of these offerings from the big companies. Also, if you see a service here that your fund doesn't offer, call and ask for it; nothing spurs a management company to make something available more than customers' letters saying this is a way to keep share-holders happy.

Here are the basic services that most investors should at least know about, even if they don't need them right now.

Automatic investment plans allow the fund to pluck cash from a bank account and deposit it into a fund. Many funds waive minimum initial investments for investors who take advantage of regular-purchase options. Furthermore, funds that have automatic plans often let you pick the day of the month or quarter when you want the money pulled, so that you can manage your deposits to fit your cash flow and the times when you have available cash.

> Note that an exchange is treated as a sale of the original fund and may trigger tax consequences, even if the exchange privilege lets you avoid sales charges.

Exchange privileges are a staple among large-fund firms, allowing you to move money from one fund to the next with a phone call, usually without having to pay any applicable sales charges.

Telephone purchases and redemptions were at one time considered state-of-the-art in customer service. Today, with on-line purchase and redemption features gaining ground quickly, they are the norm.

But there is also a subset of additional redemption features. Today, instead of cutting you a check, many fund firms will transfer the funds electronically to a bank account, giving you more immediate access to your funds. While some firms still do wire transfers—often at a small charge—that is quickly fading with the advent and growth of on-line banking.

> Some funds will send a prospectus and other documentation by e-mail instead of the usual hard-copy postal delivery.

As funds continue to develop their web sites, **on-line account status and updates** are also becoming a norm. Although I never advocate watching your fund investments by the day, week, or month (let alone by the minute), this kind of access can be handy when doing research or when you simply want to calculate your options when considering a change.

While on-line, you might want to inquire whether your fund firm will send you **electronic statements.** If you aren't reading the fund's documents—which you should—or if you believe you would keep your files better if you got all statements electronically, then consider saving a few trees and getting your documents over the Internet rather than on paper.

Cross-reinvestment, sometimes called a "**direct dividend plan**," allows you to get your dividend from Fund A and reinvest it in Fund B. It's a favorite tool of investment pros and a simple way to keep a portfolio balanced when one investment outperforms another.

Systematic withdrawals are for people who need money at regular intervals. It can be a great tool for scheduling annual redemptions from retirement accounts and a helpful way for people on a fixed income to set a budget. Because the money arrives regularly on the chosen day—monthly, quarterly, or annually—this is an easy way to get it. In addition, some systematic withdrawal programs are sophisticated enough to act as a bill-paying feature, which arranges for the money to be sent directly to the mortgage company, the bank, or any creditor with whom the monthly bill is a regular, set amount.

Systematic or automatic exchanges let you deposit a lump sum of money into, say, a money-market fund and have it pulled at regular intervals into the family's other funds. This service allows for easy dollar-cost averaging when you have a big chunk of money that you want to move.

> Keep these options in mind over time. Although some of them may not suit you today, there will come a day when they might fit your needs perfectly.

You get to select the date and frequency of the transactions (generally anywhere from monthly to annually), the amount of money or percentage of your assets to move, and where the money is going.

Asset-allocation services or programs are not common among fund firms, although some companies offer them to high-net-worth investors, which means people with anywhere from $50,000 to $250,000 minimum with a fund firm. At the low end of the spectrum, these services come with a charge; if the cost is more than a nominal fee, you might be better off hiring a financial adviser instead, as you will tend to get more customized service that way.

One other concern with these programs is that they may only allocate your money within the fund family. If the company has a great domestic growth fund but a lousy international fund, this won't make you feel good when the company suggests putting some of your money to work overseas. With this in mind, make sure you know what you are getting for your money; even if the advice is free, it can be costly.

Check writing is an overlooked feature because most people assume it is only available on money-market funds. These days, however, many fund firms groups offer check-writing privileges on their bond funds.

Direct deposit lets you bypass your bank and have some or all of your paycheck deposited directly into your fund account. Beyond that, most employers who offer direct deposit will let you split your direct deposit, so that you can have a portion of your money sent to the family checking account, with the remainder sent to one, two, or more funds. Note that most fund families will not let you make a direct deposit into more than one fund on the same paycheck. If you want to split your investment dollars between, say, two Vanguard funds, direct deposit won't get the job done since you can only have the money put toward one of your accounts.

The one thing to check in a direct-deposit situation is how easy it is halt deposits in the event that your circumstances change and you need access to cash.

Some funds offer **freebies.** Many people invest to pay for the children's college education, but they overlook the fact that their fund may be willing to provide **free education**, in the form of booklets, pamphlets, worksheets, brochures, and all kinds of other good stuff. Some fund companies offer free software packages, too.

In fact, since funds develop these goodies to be promotional materials, they will give them to you even if you are not a shareholder (because they hope you will want to become one). Call your fund company to see what they offer. If that's not sufficient, you can shop around for free fund goodies at the following two web sites: www.mfea.com (the web site of the Mutual Fund Education Alliance) and www.diansfundfreebies.com (the site for personal finance writer Dian Vujovich).

Householding is great if you, your spouse, or children have several accounts with the same fund group; you may want to save a few trees and ease the strain on your mailbox by having all of your statements (and any dividend checks) put in one envelope.

Several fund groups provide **power-of-attorney forms**, so you can grant a relative or loved one control of your assets in case you are incapacitated. Powers of attorney are a valued estate-planning tool and are frequently signed in conjunction with a will. People who already have a will may not need a fund's power-of-attorney; people without one may be able to get some peace of mind.

Be aware that if you have taxable and retirement accounts with one fund group, you need more than one power-of-attorney form. And though the forms are free, you may have to pay a fee to have them notarized.

Automatic address changes are for people who summer on Cape Cod and winter in Florida—or make regular moves between two or more locations. This function lets your statements follow you, thereby eliminating the hassle of having your mail forwarded or doing a complete change of address every few months. And while you get the statements, the monies you receive from the fund through redemptions or systematic withdrawals can either follow you or go to the bank of your choice.

THE RIGHT WAY TO PROCEED

What are you waiting for! Contact your fund company and ask which of the aforementioned services and freebies they offer, as well as anything new they might have developed. Get a thorough explanation of how the program works and be sure to ask if there are any drawbacks that other shareholders may have encountered (complaints about insufficient funds from bad timing of automatic investments, for example). Then sign up for the services most likely to benefit you.

> *Many things are lost for want of asking.*
> —ENGLISH PROVERB

DEALING WITH
YOUR FUND COMPANY

IDEALLY, YOU WON'T BE IN TOUCH WITH YOUR FUND COMPANY TOO OFTEN. The statements you get from the firm will usually be sufficient communication.

But there will be times when you want or need to deal with the fund, for example, to make a transaction, fix a problem, get new records, and so forth.

As a general rule, phone calls to the fund company do the trick, provided you have authorized telephone privileges. Simple as a phone call seems, there remains a protocol for handling situations with your funds.

> Once uncovered, transaction mistakes can usually be fixed in a heartbeat.

Any time you need to make contact with the fund family—to authorize a transaction, to check on a previous order, or whatever—pull out the file you keep on the fund. Record the date and time of the call, as well as the name of the service representative who helped you. If you are authorizing some type of transaction—whether it's moving money around, stopping an automatic payment plan, or anything else—ask for and write down any applicable confirmation numbers.

In the unlikely event of a problem, this information will make things much easier to clear up. Typically, fund companies resolve disputes in a flash. They keep copies of account forms, record telephone instructions, and have other backup systems that quickly prove what went wrong.

Many funds even fix your instructional mistakes. Fill in the wrong box and get the wrong fund, and a fund firm may set it right anyway. Some fund firms will call you trying to confirm your intentions. Several fund firms, notably Janus and Fidelity, now put fund mistakes—investments into closed funds or checks sent in where the paperwork and the amount of the deposit disagree—into the company money-market fund while they try to reach you for a resolution.

> Study every confirmation and account statement to be certain it accurately reflects your instructions. Some statements have small print on the back saying that any error you don't catch and correct within thirty days will stand as a good transaction.

No matter who is at fault, errors must be corrected quickly. Procrastinate and you could wind up on the hook for the blunder.

And with the advent of Internet trading—considered mistake-proof since the customer personally enters the data—finding your own mistakes quickly is of paramount importance.

MONITORING YOUR ACCOUNT

Typical errors occur in several areas: Monies are invested into or redeemed from the wrong fund; redemptions are made for the wrong amount; the account is registered incorrectly or with misspellings and incorrect addresses; a check for proceeds is made out in the wrong name (yours instead of some other investment company, a move that can trigger tax woes when you move retirement monies).

Your object in fixing these rare errors is to set everything straight, with no monetary or tax consequences, as if it had been done right all along. Here are the steps to follow to minimize the chance of a mistake becoming a lingering problem:

1. Keep copies of paperwork or records of phone transactions. Recording the date, time, and confirmation number of any transactions should be routine procedure. To really protect yourself, go the extra mile. Copy account applications or written instructions before sending them. This way, if you contact the fund, each of you is looking at the

> See Section 23 for more tips on fund record keeping.

same document. If you make on-line transactions, print review copies of your orders.

2. Contact the transfer agent. This is the person you reach through the fund's toll-free phone line. If the mistake involves a phone order, ask for the rep with whom you spoke originally. If the representative who draws your call doesn't have a suitable answer, ask for a supervisor. Having the date and time of your original conversation will make it very easy for the supervisor to check tapes—since virtually all transactions are made on recorded lines—with a minimum amount of searching.

"The transfer agent is going to work with you," says Terence P. Smith, president of The Declaration Group in Conshohocken, Pennsylvania, a transfer agent for several fund groups. "If they tell you that the mistake is yours, ask them to exchange paperwork; you send what you have and they send copies of what is on file. That should show who is at fault."

3. Contact the fund itself. The transfer agent works for the fund, but it's the fund company itself that should turn somersaults to retain customers.

> Most fund firms will go to great lengths to resolve almost any dispute before the authorities get involved.

This could be particularly important if you are at fault, especially with on-line trades. Perhaps you meant to withdraw $1,000 but keyed in $10,000. Some funds might allow you to fix the error—without tax consequences—so long as the extra funds were returned immediately.

It is in the fund's best interest to keep you happy so that you don't choose to take your transactions elsewhere.

4. Contact the authorities. Your state securities administrator, National Association of Securities Dealers Regulation (NASDR) and the Securities and Exchange Commission take problems like these seriously. If a problem is not resolved to your satisfaction within thirty days, make your case to people who can hound the fund to get things fixed.

You can get the contact data for your state securities administrator from the North American Securities Administrators Association web site: www.nasaa.org.

The SEC web site—which guides you through the complaint process—is www.sec.gov, and the NASDR site is www.nasdr.com.

SOMETHING TO CONSIDER

Don't try to fix things yourself. Wait for a resolution through the proper channels. If you make moves to try to correct a fund's mistakes, there may be tax consequences. Moreover, your correction might make it look as if you are acknowledging a mistake you made on your own.

Don't make the situation worse by taking matters into your own hands; be patient and let the process work before making any moves.

THE LEAST YOU SHOULD REMEMBER

Write down or get copies of every piece of information relevant to instructions you have given your fund company. Then check to make sure everything happened according to your instructions.

If it did, you can throw the supporting notes and copies out. If there's a problem, your records will get it fixed a lot faster than your memory.

THREE

WHEN YOU SELL

DECIDING WHETHER YOU SHOULD SELL

IF YOU'VE READ THIS BOOK TO THIS POINT, you should have a good idea of how to pick 'em and when to hold 'em. Now, like the gambler in the Kenny Rogers song, you've also got to know when to fold 'em.

REASONS TO SELL

Most people sell funds for one reason—poor performance. But just as performance should not be your sole reason to buy a fund, so is it a bad reason to dump shares unless it is accompanied by other factors. In general, here are the reasons to pull the rip cord and bail out of a fund:

You've reached your goals—or will soon. The idea is to have the financial control to do what you want with the money, whether it is to put the kids through college, pay for your retirement, go on vacation, or make the down payment on a house.

> If you reached the goal for which you bought the fund and are at the point where you need the money, it's time to sell (or at least get conservative with the money to ensure that it will be available when you need it).

You don't win the financial game by having the most money; you win by getting the most out of what you have. The very best reason to sell is because "it's time" and the fund has served you and brought you to where you needed to be.

You need to change your asset allocation.   Over the years, your portfolio should shift, usually becoming more conservative as you age. At times, changing your asset allocation will simply mean directing new monies into your newer choices. Sometimes, however, it will mean selling off part or all of your stake in an existing fund in order to redirect the money to a new asset class.

> You should periodically rebalance a portfolio to make sure it stays true to your mission for the money. See Section 27 for detailed advice on rebalancing.

If your portfolio is dominated by large-cap growth funds, for example, (and many portfolios are, after the bull market of the late 1990s), you may decide at some point to move capital into other asset classes (like bonds, small-company or international stocks, and so forth) that are underweighted in your portfolio.

The fund changes strategies or missions.   You buy a fund to get a certain type of asset, such as growth stocks or international investments. If the fund stops buying the sort of investments you want, it may be time look for the exit.

> Both Lipper, Inc. and Morningstar analyze and characterize funds based on what the funds own rather than on what the prospectus says they will own, so use those services to evaluate whether the fund has changed from when you bought it.

Fund companies can change holdings and objectives, usually without telling you (though you'll sometimes find clues in the prospectus). Small-company funds, for example, typically start to gravitate toward larger stocks once they grow beyond about $200 million in assets.

If you buy a popular small-cap fund, therefore, you may find that it morphs over time into a mid-cap issue.

Some fund managers make subtle changes, tilting portfolios toward hot sectors. Others ask investors for permission to buy riskier investments or to move into new asset categories. In either case, keep an eye on proxy statements and annual reports to make sure a fund has not changed its tune to something you really don't like.

Poor performance relative to similar funds.   Losses—or unexpectedly slow returns—are a big bugaboo. But a losing fund may be at the top of an ailing asset class. If the poor returns make you realize that the asset class is wrong for you, sell the shares in favor of something completely different. Otherwise, you could make the same mistake twice and stay in an investment category you can't stomach.

But if you have a long-term outlook, compare the fund to its peers to see if it's a laggard. Experts differ on how long you should stay in a fund that is consistently underperforming, though most advise between eighteen months and three years before giving up.

Try to determine why the fund is a straggler. Many superstar managers take long-term approaches that sometimes leave them out of favor with the market. You'd hate to give up on a superstar whose strategy is just about to pay off, so don't pull the rip cord until the fund really makes you unbearably nervous.

The fund gets enormous fast.   This is related to a change in strategy and mission, except that this change is often brought on by a fund's success.

Good performance almost always results in new money. Although the biggest fund groups can handle huge cash flows, small fund firms sometimes can't. If your undiscovered gem of a fund tops the charts and mushrooms, make sure the money and fame won't disrupt the manager or throw the investing style out of whack.

The fund changes managers.   A manager change should make you anxious, but there are plenty of cases where a star manager has left and the fund has barely missed a beat. The presence of a new manager by itself should not send you scrambling for the exits; it is merely a red flag. The big question you will want answered is whether the management change will alter the character of the fund.

Another red flag should go up if the fund's management company is sold. Although mergers typically enhance research power, there can be friction if a fund does not fit in with the new parent company's style. Merged fund companies also tend to combine similar funds, sometimes awkwardly, which could leave you with a merged fund that's not quite the same as the issue you bought into.

You've got a loss and want a tax refund. There are tax benefits to taking your losses, specifically that the loss can offset up to $3,000 of ordinary income or negate the capital gains taken on your winners.

If you bought the fund expecting to be a long-term investor and the fund drops in the short term, consider selling anyway—even if you expect the fund to rebound. You can always buy the fund back at a later date, but taking your losses now at least allows you to recover some of the money by reducing your tax obligations.

You wouldn't buy the fund again today. You bought the fund for a reason, maybe to get into a hot asset category, maybe to diversify, or maybe because it had a good track record and rating. If those factor evaporate over time and you can say honestly that you would not buy the fund again today, chances are that you should dump the fund. (The one exception to this is if the fund has capital gains so big that you would take an enormous tax hit in selling.)

One telltale sign that this has happened is when you stop making additional investments to the fund and can't see yourself investing more money under any market conditions. If you are a buy-and-accumulate investor, this is a sure sign that you have lost faith in the fund.

QUESTIONS YOU SHOULD ASK

Now that you know the basic reasons to unload a fund, you need to decide whether a fund that has you concerned is a "hold" or a "sell." To make that decision, run each worrisome fund through the following battery of questions. Just answering these questions periodically—even if your funds are doing fine—may help you determine how to better manage your fund portfolio.

1. Have my objectives for the money changed? You started the buying process by thinking about the purpose of the investment. Consequently, review a fund's performance by looking first at your own needs.

As noted previously in this chapter, your objectives are particularly likely to change as you near your financial goals. If you bought a growth fund but now need safety and income, you may have a bad fit.

2. Has the fund changed shape, size, or character? This is where strategy changes, management changes, and all the rest fits in. When poor performance is aligned with a critical change in a fund's makeup, you may need to rethink your investment.

3. Overall, has the fund lived up to my expectations?   One bad stretch should not turn you off a fund, particularly if it has delivered in the past. Nor should you sell a fund that has met your goals, even if it has lagged its peers. As previously noted, if you hoped the fund would deliver a return of 10 percent per year and it brings you 15 percent, don't sell it just because other funds in the same grouping have delivered 20 percent. It may still have all of the characteristics you bought it for, and it has provided better-than-anticipated returns.

4. Was the fund more volatile than I expected? You should never be surprised by what a fund does in a bad year. If a bad year for the fund is worse than you envisioned when first investing, you may need to rethink your decision.

5. Did the same things that achieved good performance contribute to the bad? What does the manager have to say about performance?   This is where a change in the fund's strategy comes into play. Most of us want a fund that's consistent, one that sticks to a discipline rather than jumping from one investment style to the next. When managers lose confidence in their discipline, it's a sign of trouble.

No one minds a fund's volatility when it works in their favor and the fund shoots up, but a fund that bounces around puts most of us on the kind of emotional roller-coaster we'd prefer to avoid.

Read up on how the manager justifies the down year, or call the fund for an explanation of what happened. Make sure that the current reasoning is sound and that you come away believing that a rebound is in order.

6. Does my portfolio need a change?   This question gets to the heart of your asset allocation. Even if your objectives remained steady and you believe the fund can rebound, look at the big picture to see if your overall investment strategy would benefit from a change.

7. Does this fund overlap with my other holdings?   If you have two funds in the same asset class and one is enough of a slacker to make you consider selling, the decision gets a lot easier when you have a second fund that has bought the same assets more successfully.

8. Would I buy the fund again today? Do I prefer an alternative?   These are always the key questions. If a fund goes through a downturn and can't recapture your complete confidence by delivering expected performance relative to its peers, it will eventually fail this test and you will move on, one hopes with better luck. If you already prefer another fund in the same asset class, you have already made your decision.

9. What are the tax consequences or benefits of selling this fund?   Even if a fund has been a disappointing performer, it may have delivered you enough growth to make you worry about capital gains taxes when you make a change. (This question does not apply to funds held in tax-advantaged retirement accounts.)

   If the gains are big enough that you have an enormous tax liability, selling may not be a viable option. You might lose so much of the money to Uncle Sam and your state (if it has an income tax) that a new, better fund would have a hard time recouping the tax bill.

> You may be able to dump a disappointing fund and improve your portfolio management at the same time.

   It's not pleasant to hold a fund that you don't much like anymore, but it may be the best decision when you crunch the numbers. In those circumstances, you may opt to sell only when you can match your gains against another loss. Conversely, when you have a loss that can help reduce your tax bill, selling gives you a tax benefit that can ease the pain of losing money in the fund. In that circumstance, you might sell the fund even if you believe it can rebound.

WRONG-WAY SIGNS

If you are selling funds with any regularity—more than one fund per year—and you are not investing based on some system of market timing or sector rotation, you are being too quick in pulling the trigger.

   Although you don't want to hold losers too long, anyone who is jumping in and out of mutual funds on a regular basis is trading in a vehicle that is really designed for holding. That's an almost surefire way to get poor returns, even if you keep making changes into the "good funds" of each new day.

MISTAKES TO AVOID

There are some times when investors sell funds they should hold onto. It can be a mistake to sell just because:

- You have reached your targets or price limits

This is trying to apply stock logic to mutual funds. Many people buy funds expecting to sell when the fund hits a certain price, assuming growth will have "peaked out" at that point.

Instead, reevaluate a fund that hits targets; if it retains the qualities you bought it for, set new goals and let it ride.

- You're trying to surf the performance charts

Don't dump a fund just because it doesn't top the annual return list. If you bail out to buy today's hot fund—tax costs aside—you may end up paying peak prices for funds that can't sustain their legacy.

> *Knowing why you should sell a fund is at least as important as knowing what to buy.*
>
> —Don Phillips, president of Morningstar, Inc.

38

DON'T MAKE EXCUSES FOR YOUR FUND

ALTHOUGH NO ONE GOES OUT OF THE WAY to find and invest in a bad fund, many people hold onto bad funds far longer than they should, enduring pathetic returns or awful treatment year after year. And since the fund world is not a meritocracy—where only funds that deserve to survive actually get to stick around—it's important that you not fall in love with a bad fund.

Sure, "bad funds and the investors who love them" sounds like a poor episode of *Oprah Winfrey*, but it's a real-life problem for many investors, where the proof lies in the billions of dollars in assets that remain in thousands of undeserving funds.

> Invariably, when you confront investors in a miserable fund, they have one of several similar excuses to explain why they stick around.

Although it is unreasonable to dump a fund after a bad quarter or two, there is no reason to stick with a fund whose yo-yo performance, mediocre returns, or downright awful behavior is unacceptable. If you have used any of the following excuses as a reason to stay in a fund that has treated you poorly, it's probably time to cut the alibis and the fund from your portfolio. It's not that any one of these problems automatically makes a fund worth selling, it's just that by the time you make excuses for your fund company, you probably have lost faith and should consider moving on.

"I'M TOO BUSY"

Inertia is your enemy. Yet people who dislike change and hate to own up to making mistakes can wind up holding a bad fund for years. Remember, a fund can be consistently awful without putting up the cataclysmic numbers that would panic you into bailing out. If you have too little time or interest to monitor your funds, don't be stunned when you wake up to lackluster gains.

"IT WAS GOOD TO ME ONCE"

Possibly the most dangerous of excuses, this is a common comment when investors have "fallen angels"—former star funds—in their portfolio. But this is a mutual fund, not a marriage partner. What the fund has done for you in the past is a lot less important than what you believe the fund can do in the future.

> If you buy the fund once performance has started to decline, it's fairly easy to get rid of it. But if you were there for some of the good times, it's a lot harder.

If recent past performance is a far cry from the glory days, don't hang on to the past hoping it will repeat itself. Decide whether you would buy this fund anew today; if not, consider divorcing yourself from the fund.

"IT'S REALLY NOT SO BAD"

Plenty of funds provide positive returns and fool investors into thinking that everything is copacetic. But if you are in the worst fund in an asset class, you could find yourself making nickels when the average fund is delivering dimes.

If you think a fund "could do a little better," don't disregard your concerns. Crunch the numbers to see whether you are worrying needlessly or whether the fund really is failing to meet your expectations.

"I'M WAITING TO GET BACK TO BREAK-EVEN" OR "I'M WAITING TO EARN BACK THE LOAD I PAID"

In either situation, you could wait forever.

Even if you recoup your losses, you might be better off getting out now and putting your money on a faster horse that speeds your recovery. It takes courage to acknowledge investment mistakes and cut one's losses rather than throwing good money after bad.

"IT CAN'T STAY BAD FOREVER"

Oh yes, it can.

This is "the gambler's fallacy," the belief that if a coin flip comes up heads four straight times, there is either a hot streak or a reduced chance that it will happen again. In fact, each flip remains a 50-50 chance.

Not every fund turns around. What's more, even if the fund does turn around, it may not be enough. Say you invest $10,000 in a fund that promptly loses 50 percent the first year you own it. The next year it rebounds and puts up a 50 percent gain. You still have a big loss (the 50-percent rebound occurred on the $5,000 you had left, bringing you back to just $7,500).

> Some funds are consistent losers for a reason, notably poor management, high expenses, or lack of discipline.

"MY BROKER HASN'T SAID TO SELL"

You want your broker or financial adviser to give you the emotional discipline to stay put and see the long view when the current market makes you jittery. But that doesn't mean abdicating the selection process or relying entirely on the adviser.

If a broker-sold fund hasn't produced results, ask why; if you get neither answers nor alternatives, it may be time to change both fund and adviser.

"EVERYTHING LOOKS FINE IN THE FUND'S REPORTS"

Of course it does. When a fund is terminally mediocre, its manager or company president puts the shine on the sewage. If the fund's statements about prospects and performance have never appeared in your account statements, then the fund may not be giving out the most accurate picture of what's going on.

"IT'S STILL GOT A GOOD RATING FROM MORNINGSTAR"

This is a cousin to "*Money* magazine (or one of its competitors) said this was a fund to hold for the next five years." Ratings and articles are snapshots, based mostly on past performance (the articles may also try to forecast which market segments will heat up). Oftentimes, they are based on long-term numbers, so that a fund with a few glorious years can live on its reputation for a long time, even after performance starts to falter.

Past performance isn't going to make your money grow over the next few decades, so ratings and past triumphs should not be the sole reason to hang on to a fund that clearly has faltered.

THE LEAST YOU SHOULD REMEMBER

If you have to justify why you still hold a fund after a period of mediocre or worse performance, decide whether your reasoning is valid or flawed.

> *To survive in the financial markets sometimes means beating a hasty retreat.*
>
> —FINANCIER, PHILANTHROPIST, AND
> INVESTMENT LEGEND GEORGE SOROS

TAKE THE
"SELL EVERYTHING" TEST

IF YOU ARE HAVING SECOND THOUGHTS about any of your mutual funds, you may be able to resolve the inner conflict by following three simple words of advice:

Sell everything now!

But before you rush out to make the phone call, be aware that this is just a test. You won't know until the end of it which funds you want to get rid of.

Start with your current portfolio. Tally up the assets in each of your funds, as well as the overall asset allocation of your money, and then move to a fresh sheet of paper.

> Simply speaking, you are going to ask yourself the question "Would I buy this again today?"

Now determine—and this could take you a while, but be thorough—which funds you would want to own if you were building a new investment portfolio from scratch. For the most part, you have the whole universe of funds at your disposal, from the ones you own now to something you read about in a newspaper or magazine.

Mentally deconstruct your portfolio and rebuild it, looking at everything from how many funds you would own and what kind of assets they buy to the weight each would have in your portfolio.

To keep this drill realistic, live within the parameters of your real life. If you invest through a mutual-fund supermarket, for example, consider only funds available through the network. If you include your retirement-plan money, don't pick funds outside of the plan unless you have the ability to move money to the investments of your choice.

The hardest part of this sell-then-rebuy exercise comes once you see the problems in your current portfolio.

Avoid too much overlap, and make sure you design a portfolio that appeals to both your aggressive and conservative sides, one that is built to get you to your goals in the time you have left to reach them.

Remember, too, that a fund that was appropriate when you had twenty years to reach your goal may not be such a good choice when you are just five years away from needing the money. Furthermore, you may have seen some of your funds do very well and may want to scale back. (Say you put $20,000 into a very aggressive fund a few years back, and the fund doubled. Now you have $40,000, and you may consider it too risky to put that much money in one aggressive selection.)

Give each fund a weighting, a percentage of your assets that it would hold in an ideal world. Then, compare this ideal-but-imaginary portfolio to your real one.

Wherever things don't match, get out your magnifying glass for a closer look.

Consider the case of my father, a man with sixteen mutual funds (down from about twenty) who hoped to both simplify and improve his portfolio by cutting down to nine.

If he dumped the whole portfolio today, his new, ideal portfolio would include just nine funds. Most would be holdovers, but one or two might be completely new. A bunch of his current funds would be gone—and his asset allocation might change.

Taxes are covered in greater detail in Sections 19 and 31.

Unless your investments are in tax-deferred accounts, selling anything or everything means paying taxes on your gains. That could be ugly. In fact, unless a fund in your imaginary portfolio is dramatically superior to something you own today, it might not be worth making a change. Size up the tax hit and project how quickly the prospective new fund might recoup that money.

You may wind up sticking with a fund you aren't thrilled with. By itself, that decision may rankle you, but in light of your entire investment portfolio, it may be easier to keep a fund that you aren't totally thrilled with when you can't find a successor that can replace it and recover from the tax hit you take.

If striving for your ideal portfolio means a change in asset allocation, you may be able to get away without selling current funds. Simply direct new monies to places where they will rebalance the portfolio rather than adding to your old standbys.

"What you wind up with is a road map," says Mark Riepe, director of the Schwab Center for Investment Research. "You get a look at where you are and where you'd like to be and the minimum number of steps to take to either implement your ideal strategy or get close to it."

THE RIGHT WAY TO PROCEED

Go ahead and take the test. "Sell" everything now and see how close your real portfolio is to your rebuilt, ideal, imaginary portfolio. Armed with that information, map out a strategy to make your real holdings more like your ideal ones.

WRONG-WAY SIGNS

If your assessment shows that you would replace your current funds only with funds that have been better performers in the exact same asset classes, you may be chasing performance rather than managing your portfolio.

Presumably, the funds you have now once looked like they had a bright future; if they look beaten now, consider whether their performance is truly bad or whether you are forever looking for greener pastures.

ANALYZING WHAT
WENT WRONG

MISTAKES HAPPEN.

Invest in funds long enough, and the odds are that you will someday buy the wrong type of fund for your goals or pursue a strategy that doesn't work, have bad timing, or just pick the wrong fund for your expectations and risk tolerance.

Typically, investors who realize they have made an error take one of three paths.

- They ride it out in the fund, hoping for a return to break-even.
- They sell the fund.
- They sell the fund and become more aggressive, investing the money elsewhere, in order to recoup their losses.

> Once you realize the mistake, the big question to ask is: "What next?"

What they most often fail to do, however, is to take a look at what went wrong.

Learning from your mistakes and making the right next move requires a thorough, objective examination of the mess you created. Doing that analysis will make the next decision easier.

Start the examination by giving yourself some credit. Assume that you picked the fund the right way, that you used the tools and knowledge you had at the time to make the best decision available to you at the time.

I make this assumption because I have never met anyone who made their investment mistakes *intentionally*. They always thought they were doing the right thing when they bought the fund, only to have the transaction turn out poorly. But between when you bought the fund (thinking it was the right decision) and today (when you are pretty certain it is wrong), *something* must have changed.

> Before doing anything with a fund that has disappointed you, focus your analysis on figuring out what changed.

In general, there are five key areas where change might sour an investor on a fund.

Look to see which of the following has changed since you bought the fund.

THE STOCK MARKET

This is the most common change, and it's also the least valid reason to make a change in your portfolio (unless the decision is made as a result of a combination of factors).

Assuming you did not buy the fund in an effort to time the market, you should be adequately prepared to understand the performance the fund could deliver in all market conditions. Chances are that you bought the fund while the market was kindly disposed toward it (most people don't buy funds in completely out-of-favor sectors).

> Isolated market moves are a lousy reason to dump a fund, but you should set some limits to your endurance. Otherwise, it's easy to get sucked into a loser's death spiral, where you ride a fund to the bottom.

If the market has turned but the rest of the characteristics that drew you to the fund are still in place, that is, if its performance is not bad relative to its peers (who would also be hurt by the downturn), its management remains in place, and you still believe the fund could be solid under more favorable market conditions, then you don't have a legitimate reason to sell the fund.

If the market's downturn has raised other issues—having to do with your risk tolerance and ability to withstand short-term losses—then a downturn could be the start of the sell process.

THE FUND ITSELF

If you have been disappointed by performance and the fund is different now from when you bought it, you have good reason to be concerned. Examine the fund to get a good idea of whether the changes are really what is contributing to your dissatisfaction or whether you are just using cosmetic changes as an excuse for getting rid of a fund when the poor performance is the result of the market.

The key changes in the fund that are likely to raise your eyebrows involve management or fund structure, mergers, investment strategy, style drift, and asset size.

Obviously, if the fund has changed managers and the new person in charge can't maintain performance at the levels you desire—or if they move the fund in a different direction, overhauling the portfolio—you have a reason to believe that the fund will continue to disappoint you in the future.

In a merger situation where one fund is combined with another, the key is which of the two funds is the surviving entity. Fund companies that merge tend to combine similar funds and keep the best track record as the survivor, so there are plenty of situations where investors in mediocre funds actually benefit through a merger. That said, if your fund is not the survivor, be sure that the new fund meets your investment objectives and follows the strategy you want.

The fund industry is rife with outrageous mergers of convenience, where two dissimilar funds are merged entirely so that the fund family won't have to shutter a fund and send everyone's money back. The fund management figures that money will stay put in these deals due to investor inertia.

Investment strategy shifts most often, but not always, to accompany mergers and manager changes. Every now and again, a fund will send a proxy statement asking to be allowed to buy private stocks, to use margin to leverage the account, or to make other important changes. If performance disappoints after a fund starts to enter new arenas, you can rightly question whether you want to stick with a changed fund.

The other big element that changes strategy is style drift, which happens when a fund—particularly one that has made its reputation buying small stocks—winds up attracting a lot of money and being forced to buy larger companies to put all of its money to work.

Clearly, asset size contributes to style drift, but it can also contribute to a general sluggishness in a fund. This is not necessarily the case—and as Fidelity Magellan has proven, "bigger" does not always mean "badder" when it comes to results—but it can be a problem, particularly for small funds that have grown large.

In all of these cases, when a fund has undergone some basic changes, it may no longer be a good fit for your portfolio. It may overlap other holdings or simply put you in parts of the market where you don't want this money to be (like government-bond investors winding up with blue-chip stocks).

In those situations, chances are it's time to move on to a fund that is better suited for your needs.

YOU

Assess whether the problem is the fund or your feelings about it, and why those feelings may have changed. The market may drive those feelings, but look at other issues, such as whether the fund is too volatile and risky for you.

Many people say they can stomach volatility, right up until the minute they actually have to do it, when they see their account value shrinking and panic.

Even if the changes are not that pronounced, most investors tend to get more conservative when they have more money to protect. That often means that a fund that was fine when you were in your twenties and thirties makes you fret when you are in your fifties. The same downturns the fund has taken over the years—which never bothered you before—now make you wince, even if the fund is still doing all of the same things that made you hold it for so long.

You have changed, and if a fund no longer fits in with your profile as an investor—it is too volatile, too wimpy, doesn't reflect the knowledge you have, and so on—then chances are it doesn't belong in your portfolio, regardless of market conditions.

YOUR INVESTMENT PORTFOLIO

Over time and with every new fund you own, your investment portfolio changes. Although you don't want too much overlap, you may grow to the point where you have more than one fund performing the same job in your holdings.

If the fund looks bad to you because of other holdings in your portfolio—if you no longer need the fund to do the job you bought it for—then there is little reason to hang on once performance convinces you that you would not buy the fund again today.

YOUR INVESTMENT STRATEGY

Many people change as they become more knowledgeable investors. Balanced funds and life-cycle and asset-allocation funds are popular first choices for investors; but as investors get older and want to take more active control of their asset allocation, these funds can make an investor feel uncomfortable and out of control.

Once you know *what* has changed, you can decide whether to hold on or to sell. And you can also be certain not to make the same mistakes again.

If you feel as though you are rushing to dump one fund so you can buy another, you could be walking into the same mistake anew. The focus must be first on the fund you own, instead of the one you wish you owned. Once you have reexamined your strategy and decided what went wrong with the fund you are dumping, you can really decide whether the next fund is a better fit or simply a replacement (in which case you could be making the same change again in a few years).

> There is a subtle strategy shift that occurs over time, when most investors tend to become less worried about growth and more concerned about capital preservation.

THE RIGHT WAY TO PROCEED

You should set limits to your downside endurance to avoid riding any fund to the bottom, either because of inertia or indecision.

Specifically, this common problem occurs when someone buys a fund at, say, $25 per share and hangs on when the fund falls to $20. When the fund subsequently falls to $15, the investor says, "I didn't sell at $20, so I won't sell here. I'll wait to recoup at least part of my loss."

If the fund continues to falter, the investor then bails out at the bottom.

To avoid the problem, set a level beyond which you will sell the fund if it keeps heading south. If you did not set this limit when you first bought the fund but current market pain has you considering a change, then determine how much more pain you can withstand before you feel compelled to make a move.

TAX STRATEGIES WHEN SELLING A FUND

THE ONLY WAY TO REDUCE YOUR TAX BILL when selling your shares is to make certain decisions *before* you actually sell the fund.

"If you want to sell a stake in one of your mutual funds, defer taxes, and have it stand up in the event of an audit, you need to know the rules and have the records before you call the fund and ask for a check," says David J. Mangefrida, Jr., former tax counsel at the Investment Company Institute, now tax senior manager at Ernst and Young in Washington, D.C.

The sale of mutual-fund shares in a taxable account generates a capital gain or loss, which is equal to the difference between what you paid for the shares and what you got when they were sold. These gains or losses are subject to taxes—even if your action merely involved swapping shares in one fund for a stake in another fund run by the same company.

> Unless the fund you are selling is in a tax-deferred retirement account, part of the selling process should be dedicated to figuring out the right way to dump your shares.

The key, therefore, is to keep track of the amount paid for a fund, including the price of shares purchased through dividend reinvestment, regular monthly deposits, or occasional additional investments. If you sell all of your shares at once, your cost equals the average price you paid for the shares. Many funds now give you this number at the bottom of your account statement, which makes the whole process pretty simple.

If you only sell a portion of your stake in a fund, however, you have three options.

Technically, they boil down to deciding which specific shares you sell, which sounds dumb because your shares aren't paper purchases but are rather a ledger entry in an electronic bookkeeping system.

The easiest way to account for a sale is to stick with the **average cost basis**.

While simple—especially if the fund firm provides you with the average cost per share—this is not usually the most tax-efficient strategy. Worse yet, once you sell a portion of your holding in a fund based on the average cost of those shares, you can't use the more tax-friendly methods to calculate your cost in subsequent sales.

> Congress has debated legislation that would make average cost per share the only way to account for redeeming fund shares but has been unable to push such a change into law.

Most often, this is the method the fund company uses for valuing your shares. In fact, when you use other methods for selling—even when you properly notify the fund company of your intentions—the average cost basis they show on your statements is likely to be handled this way (which means it could be wrong if you sell using a different method).

Therefore, if this is the first time you are considering dumping a stake in a fund, look hard at the other options before committing to average cost per share as the method of valuing your investment.

> The first-in, first-out method is the IRS's default system for figuring out which shares you sold if you do not issue other instructions.

The **first-in, first-out method** of figuring the cost of shares is exactly what it sounds like. The first shares you bought are the first ones sold. Simply look at the cost of your initial shares; if it is less than shares purchased later—which it will be if the value of the fund increased at all while you owned it—then this method will not be a great choice because it is virtually guaranteed to *maximize your tax bill if you sell a fund on which you have profits.*

As an alternative, look at the price paid for subsequent purchases and consider the **specific identification method** for determining your per-share costs.

This method allows you to pick the shares for which you paid the most money and sell them first, thereby keeping your gains to a minimum. Fund firms hate specific identification trades, because they involve extra paperwork, but you are entitled to make them (even though not every fund phone rep knows it).

There is an additional method for selling a stake in your fund that is called **average cost, double category,** but it is both confusing and highly unlikely to yield the best results. It is best attempted by an accountant with a good working knowledge of how to use it right, but have the accountant show you how it is actually saving you money on taxes, because the situations where it is the best method are extremely rare.

Now let's look at how some numbers play out: Let's presuppose that, five years ago, you bought 100 shares of the XYZ Biotech Fund in 1995 for $10 a share. Two years later, you bought 100 more shares at $25 each. The next year, the fund tanked, but you expected a rebound and bought 100 more shares at $15 a pop. Last year, the fund was up with the market, and you bought another 100 shares at $20.

Today, the price is $25, and you want to sell 100 shares.

Your total cost for 400 shares was $7,000. Your average cost per share was $17.50.

If you use the average-cost method, your gain is $7.50 per share. If you go with first-in, first-out approach, you sell the $10 shares and have a gain of $15 per share. And if you want to minimize your taxes, you sell the highest-priced shares, which you purchased for the same $25 you are now getting back, meaning you have no capital gains to pay taxes on.

Remember, too, that specific identification allows you to take a loss in a fund—even one where you have a profit based on your average cost—if the price has declined since you made one of your purchases.

Let's suppose, for example, that your second investment in XYZ Biotech had come when the fund was at $30 per share. If you sold those shares today, you would have a tax loss of $5 per share, a loss that actually can be used to offset ordinary income or other capital gains.

With this in mind, you can make tactical decisions to sell losers in order to reap tax benefits. This can be particularly helpful when you rebalance a portfolio and can manage all of the maneuvers to get a tax break (or at least keep taxes on the trades to a minimum).

Selling specific shares requires one significant change to the way you actually handle the transaction: It must be done in writing at the time you make the trade. If you make the trade by phone, you will need to submit a letter of instruction and receive a confirmation. Even then, it may not stand up to IRS scrutiny. The best way to do the whole trade is by mail, notifying the company that you want to sell, say, the forty shares you purchased in January 1998 (or all shares purchased after a specific date).

> Benefiting from tax breaks is not as satisfying as having all of your shares prove to be winners, but it at least eases the pain of having losses.

Your account statement showing the proscribed trading activity then becomes a de facto confirmation (although a written confirmation is still the best way to keep the IRS happy).

The reason for the letter is to show the fund company (and Uncle Sam) that you made your intentions clear from the start. Keep a copy of your letter, and staple it to the written confirmation you request from the fund.

If you don't have the records of your purchases, call your fund company and ask if they can provide duplicate statements, preferably long before you ever get serious about selling. Getting year-end account reviews, also, allows you to see all purchases made within a year. By saving all of your year-end statements while you own the fund, you'll have the necessary data to make the most of your selling decisions from a tax standpoint.

THE LEAST YOU SHOULD REMEMBER

If you use average cost as the basis for making a partial withdrawal from your funds just once, you must use that method with any sales in the future. You can't sell using average cost one time, then specific identification the next time.

You can, however, start with specific identification and then switch to some other method for selling the remaining shares.

Remember, too, that if you use specific identification, the numbers the fund shows for your average cost per share could be wrong in the future. The fund—even with your instructions—is likely to do its calculation based on your having redeemed the average share.

SOMETHING TO CONSIDER

One other selling strategy that can help you get the benefits of a tax loss involves swapping your losing fund for something with similar assets. If you bought a fund last year and have losses in it, for example, you can sell now and buy into a fund that invests virtually the exact same way. (But buying back the very same fund—even if you use a different share class—runs afoul of tax laws unless you wait for more than thirty days.) You get the benefit of the loss but wind up with almost the exact same assets and allocation.

THE RIGHT WAY TO PROCEED

Get your statements together and make sure you have a good accounting of how much you have paid for your shares, including any bought when you reinvested dividends and capital gains.

If you don't have records, call the fund company; it's easier to reconstruct your investment history when it's not ancient, and most fund companies are happy to help for little or no charge, provided that your request is not too difficult. Searching through the archives gets tougher every day you wait.

PULLING THE RIP CORD

ONE OF MY ALL-TIME FAVORITE STORIES of the foibles of fund investing involves a couple who didn't know how to get their money out of their fund.

Edna and Irving were facing one of those little personal financial problems that force long-term investors to liquidate holdings to meet short-term needs, so they reviewed their portfolio to see what could go and settled on the American Heritage Fund, where their remaining investment was roughly the amount they needed.

I say "remaining investment" because American Heritage—which had been a top-performing fund in 1991 but over time has proved to be one of the worst funds in existence—was in the middle of a major slump.

And so, on March 28, 1994, Edna called American Heritage to sell. But American Heritage only allowed for redemptions in writing, so the instructions and signature can be guaranteed.

Edna got off the phone, wrote a letter, and had it notarized.

A week later, she learned that wasn't good enough. American Heritage wanted a "signature guarantee," a bank or financial institution's verification of a signature's authenticity.

So she got the guarantee and mailed that in.

But American Heritage—then and now—is extremely volatile. By the time American Heritage finally processed Irving and Edna's sale, it was April 6, and the fund had lost 6.5 percent from the March day when Edna first tried to call in her sale. In total dollars, that amounted to more than $500, all because the couple did not know what they needed to do to free their money.

"We had never heard of a signature guarantee," Irving said at the time. "And to be honest, how to redeem shares wasn't something we really looked at in the prospectus. We told them we wanted to get out but lost money because we didn't know the rules."

It happens all the time.

Overall, investors don't know what's required to sell a fund. Many also overlook charges for short-term redemptions and features like telephone redemptions that some fund families require that you actively sign up for.

> Most investors put their energy into examining the reasons to buy a fund, never considering what it takes to get out.

Although the fund industry has gotten easier to deal with and problems like this are increasingly rare—and more likely to happen with small, boutique fund firms—that's small consolation if this kind of situation happens to you.

What's more, many people would never have bought a fund lacking in common exit features. Edna and Irving, for example, said they would not have purchased American Heritage had they known what was involved in a signature guarantee. But that's all hindsight for you now, because by the time you get to this place in the book, you have decided there is a fund you want to sell.

WHAT YOU NEED TO KNOW

There are five basic things to know when selling fund shares:

How do I make the transaction? Functionally, you have to know how to bail out of a fund. In most cases, telephone instructions are sufficient, assuming the fund offers phone redemptions and that you have signed up for them.

> Tax strategies for selling a fund are covered in Section 41.

If you are unsure of how you can get out of the fund, call the company's service line and ask. If you did not sign up for a telephone redemption feature, they may be able to send you the paperwork so that you can register properly. If you are selling specific shares for tax purposes, however, you may want to make your transaction in writing.

If your fund requires a signature guarantee, writing is the only option. As Edna and Irving learned, a signature guarantee is not a notarized letter. You must go to your bank or brokerage firm—some-place where they have a signature card on file for you—and ask for a signature guarantee on your note instructing the fund company to sell. The financial in-stitution will compare your signature on the letter to the signature they have on file and will then issue the guarantee (which tells the fund company that they guarantee the signature belongs to the right person).

Generally, funds do not make redemptions "in kind," which means that you get the actual underlying shares of the stocks represented by your ownership of the fund. Some new types of quasi-funds offer this feature, but about the only way your fund normally would redeem this way is in some type of mar-ket crisis or panic.

However, most funds are allowed to redeem in kind (it's buried in the fine print of the prospectus) but only in the event of an emergency, like a currency cri-sis in a single-country fund, where market instability convinces the manager that selling shares to meet your redemption would injure remaining shareholders.

Still, if you invest in esoteric, thinly traded funds that dabble in emerging markets or other potentially unstable markets, you should be aware of the pos-sibility that a redemption may not actually get your money out.

Are there any fees or sales charges involved?   There are several fees to worry about, most notably short-term redemption charges and back-end sales loads. What's crucial about these costs is that they disappear if you own the fund long enough, so you need to know how much longer they are in place in order to decide whether they are worth paying.

Short-term redemption fees generally are put on funds that are likely to suf-fer the effects of market-timers jumping in and out. They generally last any-where from three to eighteen months and can run as high as 2 percent. Some are graduated and decline when you are halfway through the minimum hold-ing period.

Back-end sales charges, however, often apply to broker-sold load funds. The investor buys in without a sales charge but faces a charge upon any redemp-tions made in a set time period (usually four to six years).

If you agreed to a back-end load when you bought the fund, you're stuck with it if you decide to sell before the minimum term expires. Most of these charges—technically known as a "contingent deferred sales charge"—are graduated, so that they may be as much as 5 or 6 percent if you sell in the first twelve months of owning the fund but scale back to 1 percent in the fifth year of ownership before eventually disappearing.

Other costs that could be triggered by your sale include "account termination fees," a completely spurious kick-em-in-the-butt-on-the-way-out-the-door charge of $15 to $25, supposedly to cover the cost of closing your account. Thankfully, most fund companies have phased these fees out. If your fund firm hasn't, complain about this charge at the same time you make your redemption, telling the fund company that it's unfair to subject you to performance so bad that you feel compelled to sell and to then pile on a fee for the privilege of leaving. Sometimes this works. Even if it doesn't, complaining on this score should make you feel better.

If you are making a partial redemption, selling just a portion of your stake in a fund, be aware of low-balance charges that could be triggered by your move. Many funds charge shareholders an annual fee of $10 to $25 if their account balance falls below a certain level.

> Supermarkets are covered in detail in Section 30.

Should your sale put you below the threshold, you'll pay this fee annually until your account grows. If you don't see yourself putting more money into this account, you might consider selling out entirely and consolidating the leftover money with another fund account where you will not face fees based on the size of your account.

Can I circumvent the charges in any way?   Some funds waive fees and back-end loads if you keep the money in the fund family. They may also give up account-balance fees if you have sufficient funds tied up in two or more funds with the company. You may also be able to avoid charges if you participate in a mutual-fund supermarket, the multifund networks run by a number of major brokerage firms.

Participating in a supermarket is also a way to get around signature guarantee requirements, as most networks take telephone redemptions that a fund must honor—even if it normally requires a written notice—in order to participate.

What are the tax consequences, and how can I reduce any tax bite?   It's important to remember that you can move seamlessly and without penalty in tax-deferred retirement accounts. In taxable accounts, however, everything triggers a tax bill, even moving your money from one fund in the family to another.

Therefore, before selling a fund, do a rough cost analysis of just how big the tax bill is going to be. If your gains are big enough and the tax hit is brutal, you may want to reconsider selling.

What happens to the money?   You have a few choices, all depending on personal preference.

The obvious selection is to have the fund company cut you a check. You may prefer, however, to have the fund wire the money directly to a bank or money-market account, an option that is generally safer and faster than having a check put in the mail.

The problem with wire transfers is that they most often are established when an account is opened; if you haven't arranged for wire transfers, you must ask the fund company for another account registration form and add this feature to your account, or you must settle for mail or a transfer within the fund company. If you use wire transfers, make sure you keep the data current; nothing messes up an electronic-funds transfer faster than the money being sent to an account that has been closed— or where the numbers have changed in the aftermath of a bank merger.

> The one thing you always can do to avoid having to pay Uncle Sam is to hold the fund.

Transferring the money from one fund in the family to another is also a fast-and-easy option, but it's only attractive if there is another fund in the family that you want to own.

If you plan to hold the money for a short time while you decide what to do next, consider transferring the funds into the family's money-market fund (assuming they have one). This keeps your money working all the time, so that you don't miss out on the days while you are deciding; the money fund will issue you checks that you can then use to move the proceeds to your next fund.

If you invest through a fund supermarket, your money usually goes to the sponsor's money fund automatically, unless you specify otherwise. If you are in Schwab OneSource, for example, your funds will move to a Schwab money fund until you move the money further; the advantage to supermarkets, however, is that you can move seamlessly from one fund family to another without the hassle of moving checks and processing new applications.

Lastly, when you pull the trigger on your sale, note the date—and the time and name of the phone rep if you do it by phone—in your file on the fund. Include the confirmation number. On the odd chance that there is a problem and the redemption is not processed properly, this gives you a chance for a speedy fix (unlike Irving and Edna's days of waiting).

SOMETHING TO CONSIDER

When you sell a fund, empty your file of all but the most important papers. Specifically, those would be your last statement from each year you owned the fund—which shows all of your purchases for the year, plus all capital gains and dividend activity—plus your confirmation of closing the account.

If the fund is in an IRA, make sure you have any paperwork related to the year and the way the fund was set up (that it shows the amount and the type of IRA you opened, for example, in 1999).

Be sure to hold the supporting paperwork for at least three years (but preferably seven) after it shows up on your tax return.

YOU'VE GOT YOUR MONEY— WHAT NEXT?

THE IDEAL RELATIONSHIP WITH A MUTUAL FUND is one that lasts a lifetime, where you hold the fund—and it grows your money at a satisfactory rate—until you have either reached your goals or till death do you part.

Statistics show that most mutual-fund relationships, however, are far from ideal, with the average holding period for funds now standing at three years or less. Since that's too short a time for most people to reach their goals—unless they are holding money in a money-market fund for some big-ticket purchase—it's safe to assume that most fund relationships end with some degree of dissatisfaction.

With that in mind, the question becomes "Why should I buy funds again?"

The answer is that unless your financial situation has dramatically changed in the years since you last bought a fund, the same basic elements that drove your purchase are still in place, and funds are most likely still the most effective tool for reaching your goals.

If you have gone through the entire ownership ritual—from buying through owning and into selling—and have only held the fund for a short time, something is wrong (and one hopes you did not go through that entire process in just a few months after reading this book).

And while I hate to point a finger, the problem could be you.

I'm taking this final opportunity to advocate that you act like an owner—like someone who is picking a life (financial) partner rather than a box of spaghetti.

245

Thinking in terms of ownership will help you select mutual funds that you can hold for a lifetime—or at least until you've reached the goals you've set for the capital.

Mutual-fund investing is not necessarily about buying next year's great fund; it's about investing in something that will serve you well for a decade or more. It's not so much about having the very best fund as it is about avoiding the worst in the bunch. It's as much about picking asset classes that you want to own as it is about deciding which of the 10,000-plus fund offerings you want to put into your portfolio.

What's more, owning a fund does not necessitate a lot of heavy lifting. It requires solid research up front, coupled with patience and periodic maintenance.

Even if you are a novice investor, you probably have more knowledge and ability for picking funds than you give yourself credit for. Take an ownership approach and there is no reason you can't find funds that will suit your needs. They may not be the top performers in the marketplace quarter after quarter, but they will produce the results you expect and measure up against their peers.

If you act like a buyer and constantly switch brands and product types—as if funds were types of shampoo or fabric softener—you are likely to wind up always looking for something better and making yourself crazy.

If you have gotten to this point—having sold funds and now having money to reinvest—throw yourself into the owner's approach to mutual funds. Benchmark your funds' progress first and foremost in relation to your personal goals and how they are helping you reach them.

Worry most in the future about how you are doing—rather than how you are *not* doing by investing elsewhere—and you will wind up with a healthy relationship with your funds. Armed with that kind of perspective, learn from your mistakes and go back to the beginning—to the very first steps of mutual-fund ownership—and reinvest your money, confident that you won't come back to this ending point again any time soon.

THE LAST WORD

I look at how my mutual-fund accounts are doing twice a year, whether I need to or not. I always wish there was more money in there but, more times than not, I like what I see.

—CHARLES A. JAFFE, SYNDICATED MUTUAL-FUNDS COLUMNIST,
Boston Globe

APPENDIX A: HOW TO REACH YOUR FUND BY PHONE

If you have questions about your fund or about any other funds, the company is only a phone call away. Most fund firms will take the time to answer even your toughest questions to get or keep your account, and many firms reward inquisitive callers with all kinds of free educational brochures and worksheets.

Don't be afraid to pick up the phone and ask questions. As an owner or would-be owner, you are entitled to fully grasp how the fund works before and after investing.

Here are the toll-free phone numbers for more than 500 fund companies. Although the list does not include absolutely every fund company out there—and phone numbers change—chances are that the firms you deal with are here.

1838 Invest. Adv.
800-232-1838

1st Source Monogram
800-766-8938

59 Wall Street
800-625-5759

AAL
800-553-6319

AARP
800-322-2282

ABN AMRO
800-443-4725

Accessor
800-759-3504

Achievement
800-472-0577

Acorn
800-922-6769

Activa
800-346-2670

Addison
800-331-3186

Advance Capital
800-345-4783

Advantus
800-665-6005

Aetna
800-367-7732

AFBA
800-243-9865

AHA Investors
800-332-2111

AIM
800-347-1919

Alger
800-992-3863

Allegheny
800-992-8151

Allegiance Funds
800-548-7787

Alliance Capital
800-221-5672

Allied Owners Action
877-575-3137

Alpha Analytics
877-257-4240

Alpine
888-785-5578

Amana
800-728-8762

American
800-421-0180

American AAdvantage
800-967-9009

American Century
800-345-2021

American Express Financial Advisors
800-328-8300

American Heritage
800-828-5050

American Performance
800-762-7085

American Skandia
800-752-6342

Amerindo
888-832-4386

AmeriStock
800-394-5064

Ameritor
800-424-8570

AmSouth
800-451-8382

AON
800-266-3637

API Trust
800-544-6060

Aquila
800-228-7496

Aquinas
800-423-6369

Arbor
800-545-6331

Ariel
800-292-7435

Aristata
800-644-8595

ARK
800-624-4116

Armada
800-622-3863

Artisan
800-344-1770

Asset Management
800-527-3713

Atlas
800-933-2852

Avalon
877-228-2566

Avatar
888-263-6452

Babson
800-422-2766

Bailard, Biehl & Kaiser
800-882-8383

Baird
800-792-2473

Baker Fentress
800-253-1891

Barclays Global
888-204-3956

Baron
800-992-2766

Barr Rosenberg
800-447-3332

Bartlett
800-800-4612

BB&T
800-228-1872

Bear Stearns
800-766-4111

Berger
800-551-5849

Berwyn
800-992-6757

Bishop Street
800-262-9565

Bjurman
800-227-7264

Blackrock
800-388-8734

Blue Ridge
800-525-3863

BNY Hamilton
800-426-9363

Boston Partners
800-311-9783

Boston 1784
800-252-1784

Bramwell
800-272-6227

Brandes
800-331-2979

Brandywine
800-656-3017

Brazos
800-426-9157

Bremer
800-595-5552

Brenton
800-706-3863

Bridgeway
800-661-3550

Brinson
800-448-2430

Brown
800-525-3863

BT
800-730-1313

Buffalo
800-492-8332

Burnham
800-874-3863

Calamos
800-323-9943

Caldwell & Orkin
800-237-7073

California Invest. Trust
800-225-8778

Calvert
800-368-2748

Canandaigua
888-693-9276

Capital Management
800-525-3863

Capstone
800-262-6631

Carillon
800-999-1840

Catholic
877-222-2402

CCB
800-386-3111

Centura
800-442-3688

Century
800-321-1928

CGM
800-345-4048

Chaconia
800-368-3322

Chapman
800-752-1013

Chartwell
800-576-8229

Chase Growth
888-861-7556

Chase Vista
800-348-4782

Chesapeake
800-525-3863

Chestnut Street
800-852-4750

Citifunds
800-625-4554

Clipper
800-776-5033

Clover
800-224-6312

Cohen & Steers
800-437-9912

Colonial
800-345-6611

Columbia
800-547-1707

Commerce
800-995-6365

Concert
800-544-5445

Conesco
800-825-1530

Cornerstone
800-322-6864

Countrywide
800-543-0407

SG Cowen
800-262-7116

Crabbe Huson
800-541-9732

Credit Suisse
800-275-4232

Creststar
800-273-7827

CRM
800-276-2883

Croft-Leominster
800-746-3322

CuFund
800-538-9683

Cutler Trust
800-228-8537

Daruma
800-435-5076

Davenport
800-281-3217

Davis
800-279-0279

Dean
800-268-4007

Delafield
800-221-3079

Delaware
800-523-4640

Dessauer
800-560-0086

Diversified
800-926-0044

DLJ Direct
800-225-8011

DLJ Winthrop
800-225-8011

Dodge & Cox
800-621-3979

Domini
800-762-6814

Dominion
800-880-1095

Dresdner RCM
800-726-7240

Dreyfus
800-373-9387

Driehaus
800-560-6111

Duncan-Hurst
800-558-9105

Dupree
800-866-0614

Eagle Growth
800-749-9933

EAI
800-798-8055

Eastcliff
800-595-5519

Eaton Vance
800-225-6265

Eclipse
800-872-2710

Ehrenkrantz
800-424-8570

Elite
800-423-1068

Empire Builder
800-847-5886

Equitrust
800-247-4170

Eureka
888-890-8121

Evergreen
800-343-2898

Excelsior
800-446-1012

Exeter
800-466-3863

Expedition
800-992-2085

Fairmont
800-262-9936

FAM
800-932-3271

Farmers
877-327-8899

Fasciano
800-982-3533

FBP
800-443-4249

FBR
888-888-0025

Federated
800-341-7400

FFTW
800-762-4848

Fidelity
800-544-6666

Fidelity Advisor
800-522-7297

Fiduciary
800-811-5311

Fifth Third
800-282-5706

First
800-442-1941

First American
800-637-2548

First Eagle
800-451-3623

First Investors
800-423-4026

First Omaha
800-662-4203

Firstar
800-982-8909

Firsthand
888-884-2675

Flag Investors
800-553-8080

Fleming
800-264-0592

Flex Funds
800-325-3539

Fortis
800-800-2000

Forum
800-943-6786

Founders
800-525-2440

Fountainhead
800-868-9535

FPA
800-982-4372

Al Frank
888-263-6443

Franklin Templeton
800-342-5236

Fremont
800-548-4539

Frontegra
888-825-2100

Frontier
800-231-2901

FTI
888-343-8242

Fundmanager Portfolios
800-344-9033

Gabelli
800-422-3554

Galaxy
800-628-0414

GAM
800-426-4685

Gateway
800-354-6339

GE
800-242-0134

General Securities
800-577-9217

Gintel
800-243-5808

Glenmede
800-442-8299

Goldman Sachs
800-526-7384

Government Street
800-443-4249

Governor
800-766-3960

Govett
800-821-0803

Grand Prix

800-432-4741

Granum
888-547-2686

Green Century
800-934-7336

Greenspring
800-366-3863

Guardian
800-221-3253

Guinness Flight
800-915-6565

Hambrecht & Quist
800-451-2597

Harbor
800-422-1050

Harris Insight
800-982-8782

Hartford
888-843-7824

Haven
800-844-4836

Heartland
800-432-7856

Henlopen
800-922-0224

Heritage
800-421-4184

Heritage West
800-576-8229

Hibernia
800-999-0124

Highmark
800-433-6884

Hilliard Lyons
800-444-1854

Hodges
800-388-8512

Holland
800-304-6552

Homestate
800-232-0224

Homestead
800-258-3030

Horace Mann
800-999-1030

Hotchkis & Wiley
800-236-4479

Hough/Florida Tax-Free
800-557-7555

HSBC
800-634-2536

Huntington
800-253-0412

Hyperion Capital
800-497-3746

IAA Trust
800-245-2100

IAI
800-945-3863

ICM/Isabelle
800-472-6114

ICON
800-764-0442

IDEX
888-233-4339

Independence One
800-334-2292

ING
877-463-6464

Integrity
800-601-5593

Internet Fund
888-386-3999

Intrust
888-266-8787

INVESCO
800-525-8085

IPO
888-476-3863

IPS
800-232-9142

ISG
800-451-8382

ISI
800-955-7175

Ivy
800-456-5111

Jacob Internet
888-522-6239

James Advantage
800-995-2637

Jamestown
800-443-4249

Janus
800-525-8983

Japan Fund
800-535-2726

Jardine Fleming
800-638-8540

John Hancock
800-225-5291

Julius Baer
800-435-4659

Jundt
800-370-0612

Jurika & Voyles
800-584-6878

Kalmar
800-282-2319

Kaufmann
800-261-0555

Kayne Anderson
800-231-7414

Keeley
800-533-5344

Kemper
800-621-1048

Kensington
877-833-7114

Kent
800-633-5368

Kenwood
888-536-3863

Keypremier
800-554-3862

Kinetics
888-386-3999

Kobren Insight
800-456-2736

Kobrick
888-523-8631

Kopp
800-333-9128

Labrador
800-494-6882

Lake Forest
888-295-5707

Lazard
800-823-6300

Lebenthal
800-221-5822

Legg Mason
800-822-5544

Leonetti
800-282-2340

Lepercq-Istel
800-497-1411

Leuthold
800-273-6886

Lexington
800-526-0056

Liberty
800-345-6611

Lighthouse
800-282-2340

Lindner
800-995-7777

Lipper
800-527-7379

LKCM
800-688-5526

LM Institutional
888-425-6432

Longleaf Partners
800-445-9469

Loomis Sayles
800-633-3330

Lord Abbett
800-426-1130

Lutheran Brotherhood.
800-328-4552

Mackenzie
800-821-4350

Magna
800-219-4182

Mainstay
800-624-6782

Mairs & Power
800-304-7404

Managers
800-835-3879

Markman Multifunds
800-707-2771

Marshall
800-236-8560

Marsico
888-860-8686

Mason Street
888-627-6678

Mass Mutual
800-272-2216

Masters Select
800-960-0188

Matrix
800-576-8229

Matterhorn
800-637-3901

Matthews
800-789-2742

Maxus
800-446-2987

MCM
800-788-9485

Members
800-877-6089

Memorial
888-263-5593

Mentor
800-382-0016

Mercury
888-763-2260

Merger
800-343-8959

Meridian
800-446-6662

Merrill Lynch
800-637-3863

Merriman
800-423-4893

Metropolitan West
800-241-4671

MFS
800-637-2929

Midas
800-400-6432

Mitchell Hutchins
800-647-1568

MMA Praxis
800-977-2947

Monetta
800-666-3882

Moneypaper
877-676-3386

Monterey
800-251-1970

Montgomery
800-572-3863

Monument
888-420-9950

Morgan Grenfell
800-730-1313

JP Morgan
800-521-5411

Morgan Keegan
800-366-7426

Morgan Stanley Dean Witter
800-869-6397

Mosaic
888-670-3600

MSB
800-661-3938

M.S.D.&T.
800-551-2145

Muhlenkamp
800-860-3863

Munder
800-239-3334

Nations
800-321-7854

Nationwide
800-848-0920

Navellier
800-887-8671

Needham
800-625-7071

Neuberger Berman
800-877-9700

New Alternatives
800-423-8383

n/i Numeric Investor
800-686-3742

Nicholas Applegate
800-551-8043

Nicholas Group
800-227-5987

Noah
800-794-6624

Nomura
800-833-0018

North American
800-872-8037

Northeast Investors
800-225-6704

Northern
800-595-9111

Northern Trust
800-637-1380

Northstar
800-595-7827

Nuveen
800-621-7227

Nvest
800-225-5478

Oak Value
800-622-2474

Oakmark
800-625-6275

Oberweis
800-323-6166

Ocean State
800-300-1116

Offitbank
800-618-9510

Old Dominion
800-441-6580

Old Westbury
800-607-2200

Olstein
800-799-2113

One Fund
800-578-8078

One Group
800-480-4111

Oppenheimer
800-525-7048

Orbitex
888-672-4839

O'shaughnessy
800-797-0773

OVB
800-545-6331

Pacific Advisors
800-989-6693

Pacific Capital
800-258-9232

PaineWebber
800-647-1568

Papp
800-421-4004

Parkstone
800-451-8377

Parnassus
800-999-3505

Pauze
888-647-5436

Pax World
800-767-1729

Payden & Rygel
800-572-9336

PBHG
800-809-8008

Pennsylvania Mutual
800-221-4268

Performa
888-800-6748

Performance
800-737-3676

Perkins
800-998-3190

Permanent Portfolio
800-531-5142

Perritt
800-331-8936

Philadelphia
800-749-9933

Phoenix Investment Partners
800-243-1574

Pilgrim
800-334-3444

Pillar
800-932-7782

PIMCO
800-927-4648

Pin Oak
800-932-7781

Pioneer
800-225-6292

Potomac
800-851-0511

Preferred Group
800-662-4769

Primary
800-443-6544

Principal
800-247-4123

Principal Preservation
800-826-4600

Professionally Managed
800-282-2340

Profunds
888-776-3637

Provident
800-618-7643

Prudent Bear
888-778-2327

Prudential
800-225-1852

Puget Sound
877-777-8438

Purisima
800-841-2858

Putnam
800-225-1581

Quaker
800-220-8888

Quant
800-331-1244

Rainier
800-248-6314

RCB
800-282-2340

Reich & Tang
800-221-3079

Republic
800-782-8183

Reserve
800-637-1700

Revest
800-277-5573

Reynolds
800-773-9665

T.O. Richardson
800-593-0134

Riggs
800-934-3883

Rightime
800-242-1421

Riverfront
800-424-2295

RNC
800-385-7003

Rockhaven
888-229-2105

Rodney Square
800-336-9970

Roulston
800-332-6459

T. Rowe Price
800-231-8432

Royce
800-221-4268

RS (Robertson Stephens)
800-766-3863

RSI Retirement Trust
800-772-3615

Rushmore
800-621-7874

RYDEX
800-820-0888

SAFECO
800-426-6730

Salomon Brothers
800-725-6666

Saratoga Capital
800-807-3863

Schroder
800-464-3108

Schwab
800-266-5623

Schwartz
800-543-0407

Scudder
800-225-2470

Security
800-888-2461

SEI
800-342-5734

Selected
800-243-1575

Seligman
800-221-7844

Sentinel
800-233-4332

Sentry
800-533-7827

Sequoia Fund
800-686-6884

Sextant
800-728-8762

Shelby
800-774-3529

Shepherd Street
800-365-6828

SIFE
800-524-7433

SIT
800-332-5580

Skyline
800-458-5222

Smith Barney
800-451-2010

Smith Breeden
800-221-3138

Sogen
800-334-2143

Sound Shore
800-551-1980

Southtrust
800-843-8618

SSGA
800-997-7327

Standish, Ayer & Wood
800-221-4795

Star
800-677-3863

State Farm
800-447-0740

State Street Research
800-882-0052

Stein Roe
800-338-2550

STI Classic
800-428-6970

Stonebridge
800-639-3935

Stratton
800-634-5726

Strong
800-368-1030

Summit
800-272-3442

SunAmerica
800-858-8850

SunTrust
800-428-6970

Target
800-442-8748

TCW Galileo
800-386-3829

Texas Capital
800-880-0324

Third Avenue
800-443-1021

Thomas White
800-811-0535

Thompson Plumb
800-999-0887

Thornburg
800-847-0200

Thurlow
888-848-7569

TIAA-CREF
800-223-1200

Timothy Plan
800-846-7526

Titan
800-282-2340

Tocqueville Trust
800-697-3863

Tomorrow
800-223-3332

Torray
800-443-3036

Touchstone
800-669-2796

TR For Credit Unions
800-342-5828

Trainer, Wortham
800-257-4414

TransAmerica Premier
800-892-7587

Turner (TIP)
800-224-6312

Tweedy Browne
800-432-4789

UAM
800-638-7983

UBS
800-794-7753

UMB Scout
800-422-2766

Undiscovered Managers
888-242-3514

Unified
800-862-3863

Unity
877-542-3863

US Global Investors
800-873-8637

US Global Leaders
800-282-2340

USAA
800-531-8181

Valley Forge
800-548-1942

Value Line
800-223-0818

Van Eck
800-826-2333

Van Kampen
800-421-5666

Van Wagoner
800-228-2121

Vanguard
800-662-7447

Victory
800-539-3863

Villere
800-576-8229

Vintage
800-438-6375

Vision
800-836-2211

Volumetric
800-541-3863

Vontobel
800-527-9500

Voyageur
800-362-7500

W&R
800-366-5465

Wachovia
800-994-4414

Walden
877-792-5336

Wall Street
800-443-4693

Warburg Pincus
800-927-2874

Wasatch
800-551-1700

Waterhouse
800-934-4410

Wayne Hummer
800-621-4477

WCT
888-592-8386

Weiss Peck & Greer
800-223-3332

Weitz
800-232-4161

Wells Fargo
800-222-8222

Wesmark
800-341-7400

Westcore
800-392-2673

Westport
888-593-7878

White Oak
800-932-7781

Whitehall
800-994-2533

William Blair
800-742-7272

Willamette
800-713-4276

Williamsburg
800-443-4249

Wilshire
888-200-6796

Wisdom
800-525-3863

Wright
800-888-9471

Wilmington Trust
800-254-3948

WWW.Internet
888-999-8331

Yacktman
800-525-8258

Zweig
800-272-2700

APPENDIX B: REACHING YOUR FUND FAMILY VIA THE INTERNET

These days, monitoring your funds and interacting with your fund company can be as easy as setting up a bookmark on your computer. What's more, many fund families offer all kinds of interesting educational freebies to both shareholders and web-site visitors. That alone makes your fund family's web site worth looking at.

Here are the web addresses for most of the fund companies that had an Internet presence as this book went to print. Web addresses do change periodically; if your fund company site does not come up based on the address shown below—or if it is not on the list at all—call and ask for the current Web address.

AAL
www.aal.org/CMC/

AARP
www.aarp.scudder.com

Acorn
www.wanger.com

Aetna
www.aetnafinancial.com

AIM
www.aimfunds.com

Alger
www.algerfund.com

Alliance
www.alliancecapital.com

Allied Owners Action
www.eraider.com

Amana
www.saturna.com/amana

American Century
www.americancentury.com

American Express IDS
www.americanexpress.com

American Funds
www.americanfunds.com

Amerindo Techonology
www.amerindo.com

Ameristock
www.ameristock.com

AmSouth
www.amsouthfunds.com

Aquila
www.aquilafunds.com

Artisan Funds
www.artisanfunds.com

Babson
www.jbfunds.com

Baron
www.baron.com

Barrett Growth
www.barrettgrowthfund.com

Bear Stearns
www.bearstearns.com

Berger
www.bergerfunds.com

Bjurman
www.bjurmanfunds.com

Boston 1784
www.1784funds.com

Brandywine
www.brandywine.com

Bridgeway
www.bridgewayfunds.com

Burnam
www.burnhamfunds.com/burnham/

Calamos
www.calamos.com

Caldwell
www.ctrust.com

California Investment Trust
www.caltrust.com

Calvert
www.calvertgroup.com

Capstone
www.capstonefinancial.com

Catholic Values
www.catholicinvestment.com

CGM
www.cgmfunds.com

CitiSelect
www.citibank.com/us/investments/

Citizens Trust
www.efund.com

Colonial
www.libertyfunds.com

Columbia
www.columbiafunds.com

Crabbe Huson
www.contrarian.com

Davis
www.davisfunds.com/

Dimensional (DFA)
www.dfafunds.com

Dreyfus
www.dreyfus.com

Dupree
www.dupree-funds.com

Eclipse
www.eclipsefund.com

Enterprise
www.enterprisefunds.com

Evergreen
www.evergreenfunds.com

Excelsior
www.excelsiorfunds.com

Fairmont
www.fairmontfund.com

FBR
www.fbrfunds.com

Federated
www.federatedinvestors.com/

Fidelity
www.fidelity.com

First American
www.fbs.com/invest/funds/faf.html

First Funds
www.firstfunds.com

First Handfunds
www.firsthandfunds.com

Firstar
www.firstarfunds.com

Flex Funds
www.flexfunds.com

Forward
www.forwardfunds.com

Founders (also known as Dreyfus
Founders)
www.founders.com

Franklin Templeton
www.franklin-templeton.com

Gabelli
www.gabelli.com

Galaxy
www.galaxyfunds.com

GAM
www.usinfo.gam.com

GE
www.ge.com/invest/in5.htm

Goldman Sachs
www.gs.com/funds

Grand Prix
www.grandprix.com

Guiness Flight
www.gffunds.com

Harris Insight
www.harrisinsight.com

Heartland
www.heartlandfunds.com

IAI
www.iaifunds.com

ICM/Isabelle
www.icmfunds.com

IMS Capital Value
www.imscapital.com

Integrity
www.integrityfunds.com

INVESCO
www.invesco.com

Investa
www.investa.com

Ivy Mackenzie
www.ivymackenzie.com

Jacob Internet
www.jacobinternet.com

Janus
www.janusfunds.com

John Hancock
www.jhancock.com/funds

Jurika & Voyles
www.jurika.com

Kaufmann
www.kaufmann.com

Kemper
www.kemper.com

Key
www.keybank.com/kfunds

Labrador
www.labradorfund.com

Lake Forest
www.lakeforestfunds.com

Legg Mason
www.leggmasonfunds.com

Lighthouse Growth
www.lightkeepers.com

Linder
www.lindnerfunds.com

Lipper
www.lipper.com

Longleaf Partners
www.longleafpartners.com

Loomis Sayles
www.loomissayles.com

Lord Abbett
www.lordabbett.com

Luthern Brotherhood
www.luthbro.com

Mainstay
www.mainstayfunds.com

Markman
www.markman.com

Marshall
www.marshallfunds.com

Merrill Lynch
www.ml.com

MFS
www.mfs.com

Midas
www.mutualfunds.net

Montgomery
www.montgomeryfunds.com

Monument
www.monumentfunds.com

Morgan Stanley Dean Witter
www.deanwitter.com/funds

Mosaic
www.mosaicfunds.com

Muhlenkamp
www.muhlenkamp.com

Munder
www.munder.com/funds.html

Nations
www.bankofamerica.com/nationsfunds

Navellier
www.navellier.com

Needham Growth
www.needhamco.com

Neuberger
www.nbfunds.com

ni Funds
www.numeric.com

Nicholas Applegate
www.nacm.com

Noah
www.noahfund.com

Nuveen
www.nuveen.com

Nvest
www.nvestfunds.com

Oakmark
www.oakmark.com

One Group
www.onegroup.com

Oppenheimer
www.oppeneheimerfunds.com

O'shaughnessy
www.osfunds.com

L. Roy Papp
www.roypapp.com

Parnassus
www.parnassus.com

Pax World
www.paxfund.com

Payden & Pygel
www.payden.com

PBHG
www.pbhgfunds.com

Perkins
www.perkinsfunds.com

Phoenix
www.phoenixinvestments.com

Pin Oak
www.oakassociates.com

Pioneer
www.pioneerfunds.com

Polynous
www.polynous.com

Princor
www.principal.com

Provident Investment Counsel
www.provident.com

Prudent Bear
www.prudentbear.com

Prudential
www.prudential.com/investing/
mutualfunds

Purisima
www.purisima.com

Putnam
www.putnaminv.com

Quaker
www.quakerfunds.com

Quant
www.quantfunds.com

Rainier
www.rainierfunds.com

Reserve
www.reservefunds.com

Robertson Stephens
www.rsim.com

Rockhaven
www.rockhaven.com

Roulston
www.roulston.com

Royce
www.roycefunds.com

SAFECO
www.safeco.com

Salomon Smith Barney
www.sbam.com

Schwab
www.schwab.com

Scudder
www.scudder.com

Security
www.securitybenefit.com

SEI
www.seic.com

Seligman
www.jwseligman.com

Sextant
www.saturna.com

SIFE
www.sife.com

SIT
www.sitfunds.com

Smith Breeden
www.smithbreeden.com

Sound Shore
www.soundshorefund.com

SSgA
www.ssgafunds.com

State Street Research
www.ssrfunds.com

Stein Roe
www.steinroe.com

Stockjungle.com
www.stockjungle.com

Strong
www.stongfunds.com

Summit
www.summitfunds.com

SunAmerica
www.sunamerica.com

T. Rowe Price
www.troweprice.com

Third Avenue
www.mjwhitman.com/third.htm

Thompson Plumb
www.thompsonplumb.com

Thornburg
www.thornburg.com

Thurlow Growth
www.thurlowfunds.com

TIAA-CREF
www.tiaa-cref.org

Timothy Plan
www.timothyplan.com

Touchstone
www.touchstonefunds.com

TransAmerica Premier
www.transamerica.com

UAM
www.uam.com

US Global Investors
www.usfunds.com

Value Line
www.valueline.com/vlfund.htm

Van Eck
www.vaneck.com

Van Kampen/Amer Cap
www.vkac.com

Van Wagoner
www.vanwagoner.com

Vanguard
www.vanguard.com

Vontobel
www.vusa.com

W&R
www.waddell.com

Warburg Pincus
www.warburg.com/

Wasatch
www.wasatchfunds.com

Wells Fargo
www.wellsfargo.com/investing/
  stgchfnd/

Westcore
www.westcore.com

White Oak Growth
www.oakassociates.com

Wilshire
www.wilfunds.com

Wright
www.wisi.com

WWW Internet
www.internetfund.com

X.com
www.x.com

Yacktman
www.yacktman.com

Zweig
www.zweig.com

INDEX

273

www.ingramcontent.com/pod-product-compliance
Ingram Content Group UK Ltd.
Pitfield, Milton Keynes, MK11 3LW, UK
UKHW051901270225
455667UK00008B/98

9 780738 202730